the Death of the Rebellious Smart Mouth Nonconformist Millennial

A Collection of Poetry from a Failed Artiste

Written by James Mitchell

Cover Illustration by Evgesha Brooks

**Dedicated to
my Grandmother Betty Hughes.
Who shared her ability to capture
the world in her words.**

*"Our world today is electronic,
Everything is supersonic.
Push a button, press a key,
London, France is there to see."*

Persona of Wrath

*How rude of me,
are you new to me & my poetry?*

*Well allow me to
introduce myself properly...*

*I'm sociopath
in a Mr. Bubbles bubble bath,
Bad at math
so I assumed the persona of Wrath,
To telegraph a maniacal laugh
as I wonder off the beaten path,
Like a Wooly Mammoth
being a sassafrass
in the aftermath,
Of a deadly auto crash
yelling out,
"Sufferin Succotash!!!"*

Over 20 Years Ago

I was introduced to the world
of Poetry over 20 years ago,
I was in 8th grade & 14 years old,
My grandma B wrote amazing poems &
I sought to follow in her
footsteps in showing &
expressing my thoughts & experiences.
It's taken many years
to find my own voice & style,
So whether you're a novice or renowned poet,
Never give up,
always express your creativity
to the world &
share your unique perspective
of love, tragedy,
life, death, struggles & triumphs.

Self Healing

As I was sobering up, opening up,
as for these wounds,
Writing was the essential instrument
for sewing them up.

Poetry

*It's the strenuous idiosyncrasies,
In construction of my poetry,
On this 20th year anniversary,
Of my 1st poem essentially,
Simplistic imagery, metaphorically,
Heart ache over love's tragedy,
Poetry inherently, infused genetically,
Graciously gifted from my Grandma B,
Continually referencing her legacy,
Of beautifying the world with her poetry.*

Hedge Maze

*Come find me in the serenity
Of our childhood days,
Playing chase me in our
Extravagant hedge maze,
"Don't leave me" was the
Last thing I heard you say,
As innocence of our childhood
Personified in the maze was
Prematurely set ablaze.*

Scavenger

What's the contingency plan,

when you swindle a man,
extract his beating heart,
scavenger shreds it apart.

Mon Amour

Coffin draped, Absentee attendees,
I mourn, no solace, Mon Amour.

Liar

Can't phantom the depth of this chasm,
As I toss in your trinkets and keepsakes
In the mist of a tantrum,
Which is conveniently
next to the withered Olive tree
with our initials carved in
always & forever,
so I added the (expletive) liar.

Sand Castle

My life is that
sand castle destined to be
washed away by the tide.

Lightening Bug

You captured my heart like a lightening bug,
Put it in a glass jar with holes in the lid,
Let it shine and brighten more than it ever did,
Showed all your friends and let them marvel,
At the sight of something so pure and so rare,
More unique than any
sentimental Hallmark card,
Love beyond measure, beyond compare,
beyond time, limitless,
Beyond yesterday, today, and even tomorrow,
Our love will be captured in sonnets, poems,
Beach shore sands,
Coupled with silhouettes
of lovers holding hands,
Star gazing at Heavenly magnificent beauties,
You'll always be my Heart,
Even if you gave me your coodies.

Love Note

Actually it's a whimsical little anecdote,
Bully's hands wrapped around my throat,
Accidently the cretin intercepted my love note,
Apparently there's an antidote
for being a love dope.

Serenade

*Strumming the melodious strings
of a mandolin,
As I serenade a love sonnet
to the damsel within,
An exquisite mademoiselle entranced
by the melody,
Relinquishing a single rose
from her adorning balcony.*

Diplomacy

*There's a time for diplomacy
And a time for ignorance,
Slap your chick on the ass
And then flick a cigarette
At your Cadillac ornament,
And I'm rather adamant
at neglecting etiquette.
that should suffice
and be quite adequate.*

Enslaved Love

*My love, why am I enslaved,
locked away in chains restrained
diagnosed to be insane,*

*My love, have I misbehaved,
dying softly from acidic poison
coursing through my veins.*

Mournful Tear

*I adhere to reserve every mournful tear,
Yet there's a deep seeded congregating fear,
To be sincere it coincides with my
mortality & something drawing near,
The feverous fear pertains to
my mother's age on her death year,
I digress to detail her early death,
But it circumvents
every attempt to avoid fearing
how many years I got left.*

Knock, Knock

*Knock, knock, knock
on the door of the catacombs,
Skull walls decorated the corridors of bones,
Spiritual entities laid to rest from a crucifix,
Demonic presence's high jinks and nasty tricks.*

Morbid Artiste

A medically induced coma,

Clinically a vegetable with bedpan aroma,
Unplug my ventilator,
Sayonara see you later,
My brain functions cease,
in other words I'm deceased,
Death of a morbid artiste,
pretentiously celebrated
as a maggot's divine feast.

Flask

It's a daunting task
drinking from a flask to forget the past.

40

Genetically fucked, pick your poison,
Mental dementia losing my memory,
Or does my mortality coincide
with my mom dying at 40.

Poetry Spark

Hi… my Dad's name is Tom,
My Mom's name is Kathy,
My name is… doesn't fucking matter,
Amongst the chit chatter
and divorce proceedings,

*I was the causality left alone needing,
Suicide note left in the tub with me bleeding,
Middle finger my signature move for greeting,
Writer's block has me impeding to finish,
My poetry spark has diminished,
I'd splatter my heart on the keyboard
but I'm squeamish.*

Miss Heroin

*So Miss Heroin,
delectable delights severed
a family member's life.
And I'm cataclysmic in retaliation
for this dramatic tidbit ya druggie chick.
Overdose, comatose, she held you close and
maliciously love to boost,
You'd never leave,
ironically she'd deceived and you left us
permanently,
Fuck you Miss Heroin,
I'm tearing in your malevolent black heart,
I'll win.*

Fright Night

*A lurid figure breathing heavy
Drops a tire iron*

& flees with his cowardice

A nursing student & mother
Beaten & clinging for her life
Lies on a street curb alone

A couple walking their dog
Notice her & administer aid
Rushing her to the hospital

A guilt stricken mother
Of the nursing student
Regrets an earlier argument

A cocaine induced frenzy
From a complete stranger
Almost left my mother dead

Brawler

Son of a bar room brawler,
Bust a bottle over your head
Leaving blood on your collar,
Son of a vandalizing schemer,
Slashing all the tires with an army
Bayonet the length of a femur.

Older Brother

*Undeniably I've been a
terrible older brother,
When the novelty of a sibling
wore off after we lost our mother,
As I reflect back on never actually being there,
Missing out on a majority of your life
as if I didn't care,
I love you brother but
unfortunately seemed I was to self absorbed,
I'm truly sorry brother for those times
that I missed or I ignored,
I could make excuses yet
that just wouldn't seem fair,
No excuse would excuse me
from this truth that I adhere,
I failed you as a brother
and for that I must apologize,
Sorry it took me
two decades to finally realize.*

Smiley

*Paparazzi crazed like
Lady Gaga exposing a ta-ta,
Fuck fame & fortune I'm broke & ill spoken,
Photogenic like a dead paramedic protesting an*

abortion clinic,
Photo bombing an upchucking Miley,
thumbs up and a smiley.

Space Cadet

Isolation aboard a space station
traversing the cosmos of space,
A Cosmonaut distraught
over a femme fatale robot,
Sabotaged the life support
& trajectory to their moon base,
An Astronaut dripping blood spots
dies from this plot,
While hurling towards a sun
finalizing the end of the human-race.

Cloud

A whimsical angel twirls from
the heavens and lands upon a cloud,
Gazes upon a lost man
stumbling through a crowd,
She whispers "look at me"
but might have been too loud,
As he caught a glimpse of a
beautiful face hiding behind the cloud.

Blue Line

Promoting a protest sign
without a sign of peace,
It's simply reads
"Fuck the Blue Line & the Police",
Trampling civilians rights,
execution on the streets,
My words secrete from a pen,
yet I'm a failed artiste.

Toad

She didn't rip my heart out,
She made it implode,
Spoiled little princess
Turned me back into a toad

Black Hoodie

Fuck Sam Goody's security detaining me,
Dumping my backpack and
searching my black Nike hoodie,
Why steal your fucking CDs
when Napster is free,
In actuality you've been
fucking stealing from me,
Extorting us teens $20 for a CD.

Lonely Birthday

Some shall announce it hearsay,
Yet tomorrow is quite a mediocre day,
Ode to another lonely Happy Birthday.

Protest

Just made a protest sign,
Smeared it with turpentine,
Said all cops are swine,
That's why I protest crime,
My antics are asinine.

Cello

Melody echoes from a Cello,
As I'm escort to the gallows,
Executioner smiles immensely,
As he blindfolds me tightly,
Preacher won't receive any penance,
I'm a Menace so I reply in defiance,
"Fuck you all" as the rope tightens,
Lesson never clash with the Titans.

Grey

Foretold was the day the

vibrant colors would erode away,
And in its absence all that was left
was the substance of grey.

Happy-Go-Lucky

Hold the thunderous applause
for being overdramatic,
But Fuck this nonsensical
bee's wax of being Poetic,
Know what I'd rather do…
some fucking Mathematics,
Like fucking formulas & equations
that are Quadratic.

Miracle

The reel of the projector spins
an image on a white screen.
A young couple being told
they'd never conceive.
Despite a miraculous miracle of giving birth,
They divorced after 2 years
casting a dark cloud over his head.
His family scorned him,
his classmates loathed him,
He was an outcast and neglected by most.
Always seeking acceptance but receiving rejection.

Why am I here?
I wasn't supposed to be in this existence.
Am I here to suffer in isolation and loneliness?
I shouldn't have been born,
I should've snuffed myself out
with my own umbilical cord.

Nobody Loves You

Nobody loves you like I do,
When you broke my heart I didn't cry boohoo
Or go cuckoo,
Just made a doll of you using Voodoo.

Mutate from Ooze

As a teenager I didn't sip the booze
or mutate from ooze,
Despite being named after a
fucking drunk Jimmy Hughes.

Pacify

Pacify the time of our existence,
In your self absorbed delinquence,
Please don't excuse the distance,
I'd still prefer our cozy coexistence.

The Good and the Bad

*As a little girl,
my mama just wanted love from her dad,
But he was to damn busy
in the bar running up a tab,
Her sisters were always jealous
of the attention that she had,
Her mama always loved her,
all the good and the bad,
I'm not sure what the attraction
the drugs finally had,
But mama chased her demons away
the only way that she had.*

Broker a Deal

*"I'd like to broker a deal" said
the antiquated distinguished antagonist,
In accordance with thievery
for longevity begs a simple naiveness,
Snarling & licking his chops
under the façade of a devoid ventriloquist,
Piercing amber eyes facilitate
a transaction of the soul for auspiciousness.*

Hanky-panky

I'd like to partake in some hanky-panky,
Since I'm obviously misbehaving,
In desperate need of a little spanky-spanky.

Under-rated

Beware of the silhouette
of Death reincarnated,
Fucking aggravated
enough to alter how the Earth is rotated,
I'm under-rated
but never fucking duplicated,
I wasn't created,
I was excreted from emaciated
stillborns with devil horns intoxicated.

Sobriety

My humblest apology
on my 10 year sobriety,
No chip to flip but
I'd prefer to pass the toxicology,
In all honesty, up all night
addicted to technology,
Fuck modesty & the nauseous
porcelain bowl recovery.

Off the Cuff

*Our mission my vixen
is to perverse the Universe,
With mayhem dispersed
off the cuff not rehearsed.*

Enchantress

*All hail to my enchantress,
Sexcapades on the mattress,
Seductress in a slit dress,
A masquerade's temptress.*

Endless Summer

*And I only dreamt of an endless summer evening,
Wrapped in your arms content,
no disbelieving,
Sunset softens your face
as we kiss before leaving,
Pondering our love,
anxious about our next greeting.*

Underwater

*It's like I'm drowning underwater
never surfacing,*

Sharks circling, I'm panicking,
the lights darkening,
The past's weighing me down,
Death is whispering,
"Come on mate, give in,
let go of all your suffering."

Beyond Belief

Hers is a story beyond belief,
Being beat, left unconscious,
bloody in the street,
Being sexually assaulted by a stalker
(a line I wanted to delete),
Being abandoned,
losing custody of her son,
but never accepting defeat,
Being rejected by family,
ridiculed and shunned as the black sheep,
Being mistreated to being diagnosed
with a weak heartbeat,
Being addicted to drugs and alcohol
trying to feel complete,
Hers was a story beyond belief,
Being my Mother I'm proud of her,
she was the bravest woman
you'd ever meet.

Cockamamie

*Let's me introduce you to
the zany cockamamie,
A zombie Harry Caray taking a selfie,
While pissing on a Chicago Cub's Tee,
'Cause to me,
I got a better chance of licking
the whip cream & cherry off
of Katy Perry,
Or leaving bite marks
on Ronda Rousey's dairy aire,
To the contrary, I'll never be Legendary,
Or get a million likes for shitty poetry,
Like R.M. Drake & his talentless Fuckery.*

Alcoholic's Anonymous

*Excuse me Alcoholic's Anonymous,
But your girlfriends' a hippopotamus,
Or an elephant with ginormous tusks
with impaled male carcasses.*

Anarchy

*A cumbersome cynic
that mimics sexual addicts
& late night debauchery,*

*A troublesome hooligan
high on hallucinogens
from a pharmacy robbery,
A bubblegum lollipop
princess accompanies
in a nonstop
state of anarchy.*

Words Have Depth

*You felt the heart
behind my Grandmother's poetry,
Unfortunately she wasn't able to
share it publicly,
Yet she inspired me
to write and think creatively,
Have my words have depth,
ceasing your breath,
Clutching a rosary as an evil entity
teases you with Death,
Like the warning being ignored
from a demonic Ouija board,
Inciting an evil horde to gored
everyone that you've adored,
Escaping the mental ward
with the cassettes of
therapy sessions they'd record,
And erasing those mother fuckers*

so the norms thought your sanity
was restored.

Zack Morris

I repeat myself more than
a Fall Out Boy chorus,
Just like Screech
I idolized Zack Morris,
"Sharrup you mouth!"
like Bullwinkle's Boris,
Don't make me kick your ass
like 80's Chuck Norris.

I'm Not White

Idiot, I'm not white;
I'm just color deficient,
An insignificant blue eyed
ambitious miscreant.

Insecure

A good-bye letter titled Insecure
So apprehensive
I left out my own signature.

Menace

I've been a menace, a masochistic dentist,
Mechanically laughing at
Cabbage Patch Kids eating lettuce.

Set Asunder

Foretold in torn sheets of dried ink,
The tale of a quivering lip unable to speak,
Of a gentle tear uprooted from a teary eye,
A dawn immersed in a mother's lullaby,
As a son witnessing her eternal slumber,
Good-bye dear mother, we've been set asunder.

Black Hole

Speculating if my heart had a black hole,
Bridging the gap between that & a lost soul,
She's a celestial beauty emitting true love,
Touch by an angel, my savior from above,
Birth me a child that made my heart whole,
& married that mate that reunited my soul.

Problem Child

Back when I was a little tike,
I use to peddle bike,

*Up & down the block until it was night,
Even host a scar from my 1st rock fight,
I got it from Cheeseball
this kid I didn't like,
Problem child of the block
would explode like dynamite,
As soon as the lamp post flickered light,
I'd be in the house avoiding
that ass whooping fright,
Playing with my night bright,
Thinking about the words I might,
Display as a good night.*

Mother, I Love You

*I was standing in the
kitchen at age eleven,
Afternoon sometime maybe
a quarter to seven,
My dad told me
my mom almost went up to heaven,
Overdosed on heroin,
saw the bright light almost went in,
Told me to dial her up,
tell her I love her,
ask her to sober up,
I cried sobbing teary eyed,
Mom I don't want to lose you,*

I don't want to see my mom
in an early grave,
Mother I love you.

1st Lesson

1st lesson in deception
was a fatal attraction,
High school antics,
a couple of romantics,
A couple roses but
never made it to the mattress,
A love addiction
better than fiction that backfired,
Both going haywire,
hearts caught in a cross fire,
Neither apologetic,
the same old rhetoric,
1st love was a misconception,
best off not to mention.

Lost Poetry

I dedicate this poem
to all those poems
crumbled up and tossed away.
All those poems
deleted or never finished.

*All those poems
never read or published.*

Hodgepodge

*My writing is hodgepodge
of the unconventional,
With a hint of intellectual,
a tad bit of conceptual,
Yet the subject matter may
not be socially acceptable,
Is it a masterpiece or another item
for the trash receptacle.*

Welcome to Heaven

*The paramedics couldn't resuscitate,
So I ascended to the Pearly Gates,
Surprised to see the Devil
there to congratulate,
You're so hated not even your family
or friends will congregate,
Absentee attendees at your wake
but by any rate,
You selfish little ingrate,
Did you know it's rude to make
the Devil wait?*

Manifestation

I'm the manifestation
of those thoughts of suicide,
That you meticulously try to hide,
The insatiable pain you politely deny,
As you cordially invite
Death to pass you by.

Lobotomy

Mother fucker,
try dealing with my family
You're better off getting
yourself a lobotomy.

End of my Book

Disorientated & panicking
as I can't grasp air in my lungs,
Face twitching like a stroke
expiring am I finally done?
Fiancé dialing up 911,
my heart beats racing
as the ambulance comes,
Oxygen and IV hook ups
and speed racing to Mercy Hospital,
"Take these aspirin chewables"

*Are these my last fleeing
moments on Earth,
I look over at my fiancé
praying to God don't let
this be the end of my book.*

Sleeping Sheep

*Sitting alone in the high school cafeteria,
No friends guess I didn't fit the criteria,
Getting hit by jocks but not
fists it's tater tots,
Some girls giggle
but I react like a deactivated robot,
Slowly bury my head into
my elbow acting asleep,
Daily routine fuck school
won't conform like the sheep,
From elementary to
junior high to high school,
Never had friends
never been considered cool,
Spit in my face, punch to the chin,
knee to the gut,
Go home chased, I'll never win,
slam the door shut.*

HANDLE WITH CARE

I'm not sure if you're aware,
But the label on my heart reads
"HANDLE WITH CARE".

Silver Spoon

Grew up spoon feed amoxicillin,
Wasn't born with a silver spoon I assume,
It was used to shoot up heroin,
By my drug addict parents all afternoon,
No walks in the park no big red balloon.

No Consequences

Hypnotized by the loud heavy metal music,
I'd use it to focus the pain
into a focal point,
No smoking joints but dulling my senses,
No consequences I'd cut into my forearm,
Participate in self harm
with a kitchen knife,
Fuck my life dealing with
losing my mom at 14,
No self esteem heart
felt ripped at the seams,
Nightmarish dreams of Death welcoming me.

Family Values Tour

A bit of a blur, how did it occur,
fell in love with her,
I was so unsure, fucking immature,
cocky demeanor,
Maybe that was the allure,
thought I was the shit like manure,
Family Values Tour,
higher than Harold and Kumar,
Back of a police car, door ajar,
Caught red handed
with my hand in her cookie jar,
I'll try not to censor
the rest in my memoir.

Little Piggies

Yelling "Fuck You"
to two skin heads in an Escalade,
Peeling away as my middle finger waves
like a renegade,
Cop lights flashing
turns out that fucking Escalade,
Had two enraged little piggies
hot as bacon sautéed.

Re-Edit

Greetings,
I use to be my Mamma's little Sunshine,
Tearing up now so
let's sharpie over that last line,
Better now so
I'm a mad scientist's design
of an asinine Frankenstein,
Of Dead Poets reenergized by
a battery that's Alkaline,
A love addict
"Won't you be my Valentine?"
as I plummet off of Cloud 9,
A Goddess so divine
I'd trade in my straight
jacket for a suit & tie,
& re-edit my tragic suicide
for a Happily Ever After
kinda storyline.

Strung Alone

Strung along, I'd sing along,
To your favorite love song.

Who am I?

Who am I?
Say Good-bye
A specter of torment
A life that is dormant
Kiss Good-bye
Who am I?

Best Friends Forever

When I was sixteen
I was so sure
we'd all be best friends forever,
Even insisted my Dad was wrong
that'd we wouldn't last forever,
You guys were my best friends
until we slowly parted ways forever,
Even right now
we never talk despite the fact
I'll miss them forever.

Feeling Alone

Miserably I walked alone for so long,
Hated myself and everything with it,
Wanted to silently kill myself but
Just didn't have the strength to do it,

I made sorry excuses for the mental abuses,
Hating my parents even when my mom died,
I felt alone, so very alone, no friends,
Felt hated by my family and alone,
An outcast in my very own family,
So alone the only way out
I felt was to die alone,
But as time passed,
I didn't feel so alone,
And that suicide feeling died inside of me,
I was finally free to find
that happiness inside of me,
And I wasn't alone;
I finally had a family that loved
and cared for me,
And I finally didn't have to
walk all alone.

Abracadabra

Fucking abracadabra
here's proof of my authenticity,
As a socially awkward teen
struck by electricity,
Sparking a fight that
would insight word babble,
The hawing & humming,
I'm just a rabble-rouser,

Fucking amateur,
I'll the saboteur of insults & slander.

Evil Horde

Fucking Snapchat
how do I record,
The evil horde
I'm about to unleashed
from this Ouija board.

Poetry Corner

I want my poetry narrated by Tom Waits,
In an dingy obscure poetry corner
while Ralph Steadman illustrates,
All the while the audience contemplates
whether to congregate
or hastily evacuate,
From the inner and utter pandemonium
my collection of poetry creates.

Pour My Heart Out in Secrecy

I'd pour my heart out in secrecy
in the entries of this diary,
Dear Diary,
I owe you an apology

for this is my last entry,
I'd call her religiously
every single night you see,
Probably just to have her comfort me
from my life of misery,
I had no friends you see,
and life wasn't set on easy,
I selected the highest difficulty;
luckily Mom was there for me,
And one night you see,
the night I didn't call
God took her from me,
And regrettably,
I'll never have closure
to move on you see,
I was only fourteen,
and now I'm thirty five
sharing my final diary entry.

Memorable Memento

It's fucking exhausting prying these nails
out of my fucking coffin,
And it isn't often I fucking apologize
'cause my hatred never softens,
And here we fucking go, I'm fucking sorry I
obliterated your ego,
Allow me to extract my heart

from my torso and bestow it to you
as a memorable memento.

End of Our Sessions

Psychologist:
I think it's time we end our sessions.

Me:
End, we didn't even fucking begin,
Even scratch the surface or find my purpose,
My mind's a fucking disaster,
You want to put me out to pasture,
Dastardly thoughts please fill in the dots,
I'm about to unhinge and binge watch every episode
of Shameless,
And write cliché poetry till I'm Fucking Famous.

Thunder's Crescendo

Beads of rain trickle down
the wooden framed window,
Searching the gray clouded sky
that encompasses limbo,
Magnitude of a loss
accompanied by the thunder's crescendo,
Descending into loneliness
yet finding strength to continue.

Agree to Disagree

Doc,
I'm immune to your psychedelic hypnosis,
I'm pretty much fucking hopeless
in this psychosis,
Let's just agree to disagree,
#Fuckyourdiagnosis.

Reader's Digest

Fuck Reader's Digest and its obscure
cozy corner of happiness
in an article about
"What it's like to be depressed",
It's like your minds mechanical gears
malfunction leaving your inner mind
a fucking Hoarder's mess of inconsolable fears
to manifest from vivid nightmares
an avid reader couldn't possibly digest.

My Future is Hopeless

It's personal
so I'll bash your
fucking head against a
urine stained urinal,
Eternal damnation that my

*note pad is immortal
but my carcass rots
leaving the Earth unfertile,
A vicious family circle
suffocating each other
as they're gasping for air
until they turn purple,
I'm a distorted
aborted fetus with tuberculosis
clinging to life
wearing a onesie with reads
"My Future is Hopeless."*

Completely Septic

*They say
"blood is thicker than water"
except when it's acidic,
Because plenty members of my family
are basically parasitic,
Overly narcissistic,
alcoholic and vengefully
they're sadistic,
I was even a tidbit skeptic
but there's no cure for a
mind that's completely septic.*

Piss Poor Attitude

About this piss poor attitude,
I ripped the catheter out of my urethra,
After a local anesthesia,
partial amnesia,
Hi… it's nice to meetcha.

Megalomaniac

It's the return of the megalomaniac,
A hypochondriac digesting Xanax
for panic attacks,
My sexual appetite is insatiable
and I'm incapable of paging
Dr. Heathcliff Huxtable,
'Cause he prescribed generic Quāāludes
to get Raven-Symoné in the mood,
And fuck Bill Cosby Dude,
I'm cosplaying as Fat Albert in the nude,
#Moobs on Twitter battling that noob
Jessica Nigri who's got the bigger boobs.

McGruff

Never admit that you're brain damaged,
Or savage enough to get bound and cuffed,
Or high enough to get arrested by McGruff,

Face down in your old high school crush's muff.

Empty Bottle of Whiskey

*Do you fucking miss me,
empty bottle of whiskey,
Sat up till a quarter to three,
Seriously what the fuck is wrong with me?*

Easier

*They cordially say
"Greif gets easier with time",
Let me clarify that pretentious
assumption with mine,
On the verge of the 19th anniversary
since my mother died,
Undoubtedly not enough buckets
to hold the tears I cried,
And as life's chapters unfold
there's a common theme,
I mourned the lost of my mother
and lost self esteem,
Delinquency along with
alcohol dependency elicited me,
To grieve in resentment
for what God has stole from me,
As I linger in a cemetery*

stumbling to her tombstone,
I sip from a flask
remembering a past of being alone.

Kubrick

After foraging for weapons in police storage
in the City of Florence,
& having Lloyd giving shots to me & Jack Torrance,
Drunk driving with Florence Henderson
hitting 4 inch orange cones
& winding up at a diner
being spoon feed cold porridge
Watching a Clockwork Orange.

Cherry Coke

I'm a boarder line schizophrenic,
Escaping a mental clinic,
Or was it a picnic,
Drinking acidic Cherry Coke for aesthetic,
While dressed as unsympathetic paramedic,
I'm particularly a pathetic male specimen
That's possibly photogenic, it's genetic.

I Forgive You Mom

Each day when the sun shines

*It reminds
Me of a time when I had everything
And I feel so alive
Not any butterflies
Prepared to take a dive
Into the unknown
I've made my own home
Reinforced it with the
strength of my back bone,
I forgive you Mom,
I wish you were here,
I'm proud of you and no need to shed a tear,
I'll always have you in spirit so be free,
To find happiness
like the happiness you've shown to me.*

Genesis

*As I attempt to dictate
the scribble scrabble note page,
Of a love story between
a delinquent couple of teenage,
Star cross lovers intersecting
in a chance encounter,
A lonely hitchhiker welcomed in
by a night time driver,
I'll reference them as
Mom & Dad for the remainder,*

*Of a insignificant tale of an
offspring's mild disclaimer,
A love vessel wreaked by
turbulence I'll emphasis,
Even Adam & Eve scorched
Paradise in Genesis.*

Peppermint

*As soon as I tasted her sweet lips of peppermint,
I had to reduce my time spent
into smaller increments,
Of hanging out with my rambunctious group of
miscreants,
Which was quintessential
to establishing
my good guy embellishment.*

Soul's Burning

*Give me that influential clarity,
No hand outs fuck your charity,
Desolated in Hell's own disparity,
Still sorrowful the knife is dull,
Suicide note is still in my skull,
You'll be delightful I'm so spiteful,
Heed my warning before the morning,
I'll leave a reason for your mourning,*

Still yearning yet my soul's burning.

Cool Guy

*Attempting to circumvent
being that nobody nerd freak,
Into the impeccable cool guy
witty with the tongue in cheek.
Braces & glasses out of rotation
but still not flavor of the week.*

Blind Eye

*Seems to me those cops always turned
a blind eye to the underage drinking,
Drug dealing, gangbanging
but don't let them catch you skating,
then you're a juvenile delinquent,
a figment of rebellion in a functioning
societies ideology of cultural norms
like opening up a can of worms,
just another excuse for corrupt
criminal lawyers to fill out legal forms,
the Death of the Rebellious Smart-Mouth
Nonconformist Millennial
just to conform.*

Never Hear

Fuck it;
I'll provoke the spirits that I'll inherit,
The merit to speak rhymes
to an audience that will
undoubtedly never hear it.

Stare

I defeated some Care Bears
in Time Square with the
"I don't fucking care" stare.

Day You Died

Tremendous void inside
Become personified
Deprived of tears to cry
That day you died.

Magician

If I were a magician my mission
would be to boost up my reputation
and be exhilarated from repetition
of poetry's limitations.

Comic Strip

More offensive than a Boondocks' comic strip,
Instagram told me to
"Zip my fucking lip",
Refresh your page
if you can't decipher my sloppy penmanship,
Or has it's been deemed
inappropriate by Instagram
for blatant censorship.

Interference

Once in awhile I'd like to throw in
a little interference,
Say how I actually feel sometimes
like "Fuck my Parents".

Solitary Confinement

I sentenced myself to solitary confinement,
Pathetic now-a-days movies are
my only excitement,
It's like my life turn dormant
to avoid pain and torment,
Deep seeded depression
turned into abandonment obsession,
Feels like anyone I'm close to

leaves or passes away,
Like God decided I never deserved
perfect happy little day,
I don't exist to my family,
my friends they've abandoned me,
Keep searching for the strength
but it keeps coming up empty.

Blank Verse

If only I could traverse
to an alternate universe,
Get immersed back in '97
and attempt to converse,
With my nurse Mother to adverse
and/or reverse,
Her death curse so this poem would
become a blank verse.

Decoration

She took the mangled pieces of your heart
And mushed them into a decorative art piece
To gather dust on her book shelf
of tragic love.

Night Light

*Go ahead and laugh but I use to sleep
with a night light on,
Didn't know why until my wife
noticed that evil demon,
Floating 3 feet above me
whispering to me as I slept,
Even in my dreams he tries to kill me
a little secret that I've kept.*

1982

*Mother Fucker I was born way back in 1982,
I'm thinking my 1st words were "Oh, Fuck You",
Fuck authority
I've been disobedient since preschool,
Fucking potty mouth I was the
equivalent of a juvenile Deadpool.*

Dear Whomever

*Dear Whomever,
Sorry to be too vague in this endeavor,
Just a subliminal attempt at being clever,
Trying to quell this jubilation from anger,
Let this mundane expression linger with a middle
finger.*

Crying at Night

Don't misconstrue the context of a text,
Don't conclude the night
crying with a box of Kleenex.

Worth Saving

Hyperventilating as I'm self medicating,
Rooms spinning or am I fucking levitating,
It's devastating my body's degenerating,
I'm contemplating if my life's worth saving.

Dear Mom & Dad

Thanks for not making it till my 3rd Birthday,
Guess being selfish and
having a kid could get in the way,
With all that partying, drinking,
and drug using,
Guess reading books and
singing songs wasn't happening,
Thanks for putting me in the middle
of your custody battle,
Pretending you each wanted me
was all just fiddle faddle,
Thanks for preparing me for a life
of sadness and tragedy,

Who could've predicted your death Mom
and Dad's marital regret
for breaking apart our family.

Brain Goop

My brain turned to goop
and it just oozed right out
Any normal person would have
freaked the fuck out,
Fuck being mentally alert
I rather wonder aimlessly about,
And spontaneously shout out obscenities
like shut your fucking mouth.

Carousel

It just dawned on me,
that I publicly,
disclose my inner thoughts
in the form of poetry
Go ahead, lock me up and throw away the key
It's plain to see these
confessions from a padded cell
I'm compelled to tell my fond readers
I wish you all a fond farewell,
Now allow me to reap the benefits
of riding my imaginary carousel.

Brand X

We extracted Brand X from everything nice,
Generation X taught us to never think twice,
Fuck the entire world and
throw a middle finger up,
Drink and party up in here
till we're throwing it up,
Anti-Everything Mother Fuckers
respect for nothing,
We're the bastards of drug addicts
that left us with nothing,
But that pure rage and anger
got sedated and medicated,
The message of revolt
turned into brainwashed submission,
And all of us early Millennials
lost our fucking Revolution.

Mad, Mad Doctor

A breathing apparatus
filtering toxicities in the air,
As the mad mad Doctor extracts his satanic heir,
Hence my son shall bear the name of Armageddon.

1st Show

*Adrenaline and nervousness
on the night of our 1st show,
1st performance live so best believe
we invited everyone we know,
We practiced for 2 years
and even recorded a 3 song demo,
Called it Love Fest location
Marvin's basement read the memo,
And as 100 plus awaited us to
start up this musical show,
I glanced out and noticed
you weren't in the front row,
So I stalled until you arrived
but the cops busted up our show,
Afterwards band broke up
and never got to give it another go,
But the only consolation is
we're married and it was worth it so,
'Cause you were the only one I wanted to
sing for at our 1st show.*

Rubbish

*It's true I may never be published...
But at least my poetry
isn't a bunch of fucking rubbish.*

Pompous

Relax chum, just rewire my cerebellum,
The outcome my brains numb,
And you can dislodge the pompous stick
out of your rectum,
The boredom of the humdrum
mundane life of a dumb beach bum,
Chewing Rum flavored Bubblelicious bubble gum,
Skinny dipping in a shark infested aquarium.

Little Envy

Shades of green little envy,
Miniscule heart that was empty,
The darndest kisses often deadly,
Let me surrender to it gently.

Clumsy Words

My humblest apology for no poetry today,
My mind had a short circuit
causing my idea light blub to burst,
Leaving my thoughts to disperse,
After a slew of curses, nonsensical verses,
I deleted my clumsy words & said,
"Fuck it, I'm done",
Scrunched up my face &

continued reading Ready Player One.

Rebuttal

But my Dad said,
"I still managed to fuck up my life
without being a drug addict or alcoholic".

Yet I have a rebuttal,
can I be perfectly blunt than subtle,
It's hard to follow in your
drunken footsteps Dad,
If I had I wouldn't have been a college grad,
I would've sat on a bar stool flustered and mad,
Blame everyone else for my shit life,
oh woe is me, I'm sad,
Yet instead of emptying my pain
in a bottle I used this note pad,
And if I failed at things
I attempted well at least I tried Dad.

Misery's Company

Accompanied by Misery,
We are old friends,
She led me to sanctuary,
Amongst those condemned,
At the cemetery I was buried,

She was the only one to attend.

Meticulous

So meticulous, I scrutinize every single line,
I divulge myself till my heart,
pain & spine intertwine,
Heart palpations as words
emerge with paper & combine.

Clumsy of Me

How clumsy of me, did I just break you heart,
Pieces clogging up my vacuum breaking it apart,
Now the mother fucking thing won't even start,
Oh shit, are you still here?
Wait let me say some magic words
like Abracadabra so the fucking crowd
will cheer when you disappear.

Mister Pathetic

Salutations, my name is Mister Pathetic,
No need to panic just relax with a Xanax,
I'm a slumbering bumbling walking cliché,
Writing clever little haikus
while sitting on a bidet.

Eradicate

My heart takes the daunting task of falling fast,
Sips from a Whiskey flask to eradicate the past,
Cordial as we reveal our masks & hope it lasts.

Bridging the Gap

"Love is like a roller coaster,
First she pulls you closer,
Then puts your heart in a toaster." - '97

"An unreciprocated love like Scully & Mulder,
Her dream man hangs above her bed,
a Mark McGrath poster,
While she plays games like Dream Phone,
you'll have closure it's over." - 17

Off Getting High

Dear Absentee Parents,
off somewhere getting high,
I'm one of the forgotten 80's kids
somehow I survived,
I was raised by grandparents
while you off getting high,
The cocaine, the heroin and alcohol
promises and lies,

Pretending to give a fuck
while you were off getting high,
My fading memories of your
overdoses and heartfelt hugs,
Now our visits are at a cemetery
where your grandkids say "Hi".

Be Her Valentine

Don't be asinine,
she'd never ask me to be her Valentine,
Not even in a desperate act of being kind,
I'd get shot down faster than Columbine.

58th Fairfield

I fucking grew up on 58th Fairfield,
Skateboard deck was a bit peeled,
80's youth without that
pansy-ass safe-space shield,
Scars that haven't yet healed,
A hard fucking life
recorded in my Trapper Keeper
never to be revealed.

Star Was Born

Mom, they never said a star was born,

The fateful day that you came into this world,
All alone I've mourned,
That your light grew too bright
for this selfish world to adorn.

Pretentious Smiley

Why do you even like me?
I hide behind a fake pretentious smiley.

Primary Excuses

My brain waves are getting distorted,
spines contorting,
Primary excuses' just blame it on
the drugs my parents snorted.

Lazarus

I'm a cancerous Lazarus in damnation
for being an atheist masochist,
A suicide activist with bandaged wrists
in the Military line to enlist,
A non-recognizable narcissist artist
that never recovered from jaundice.

Overweight

As I kid I use to be embarrassed of my parents,
Imagine your Mom in the 90's being overweight,
With constant jokes like
"What's Eating Gilbert Grape",
And "Your Mamma's so Fat…",
How's a socially awkward kid
suppose to handle that,
And the fact my Dad was the trash man,
Tossing out the trash,
I was a bit apprehensive
about disclosing all of that.

Nerdiness

Her adjacent locker stores
her cheery pom poms,
She snickers at my nerdiness
like a teenage sitcom,
When up walks her muscle head dreamy icon,
Who shoved me out of the way but
I'll let bygones be bygones,
Besides whoever heard of a
nerd & a cheerleader joining atomic ions.

November 5th

It all culminated on November 5th,
A cosmic shift, continental drift,
A parallel rift, an unholy gift,
What ensued was the devil was about to undo,
humanity with the birth of a child
in the year of 1982.

Mantra

You left my heart encased
in ice like the frozen tundra,
I repeat your final words
"I don't want ya"
like an obnoxious mantra.

Faulty

The video flickers in and out
like an old V/H/S tape,
You're smiling, dancing,
and there's happiness in your eyes,
The audio is faulty at the moment
you say you love me.

Uproar

An upheaval, an uproar,
of laughing as my pants hit the floor,
Pulverizing numskull bully
depantsed me once more, Skinny ankles,
squeamish knees under whitey tighties,
Exposed for all these rambunctious dolts to see,
Maybe tomorrow I'll wear my smarty pants
with one of these…
Middle Finger Up

To Be Happy

I use to wish to be happy,
Gee what would that be like,
And it wasn't until I had a family,
That I experienced it with
my children and wife.

Mock Me

Ode to the pimply teenage days of those
oodles of puss filled zits,
Applying Clearasil to no avail,
I have a little secret
if you promise to keep it,
I'd apply makeup concealer

& not apply it properly,
So the kids at school
would constantly mock me.

Healing Scars

Let's douse the flames,
Sifting through the ashes,
Of a past burned away,
I relinquish my name,
Healed scars from lashes,
Enabling me to walk away.

Revisit

Futile to portray a broken home,
Insubstantial imagery in a poem,
Hesitant to revisit all those gone,
Childhood evanesces as I look on.

Tree Surgery

I got a college degree
to take a chainsaw to a tree,
No PhD but I can perform a
fucking tree surgery,
Grand Daddy would be so
flipping proud of me,

*I followed in his footsteps
now I'm working in Forestry.*

Walls

*I built these walls around me,
Somehow you surprised me,
I let you inside to finally see,
What this life was like for me,
Your love began to comfort me,
Those walls came down slowly,
& when I trusted you completely,
You eventually just abandoned me.*

Pure

*I concur that my poetry detours
A larger audience with
proper vernacular,
I accepted that I'll remain obscure
But let me assure you
I'll remain pure and spectacular.*

Permission to Return

*Heaven please grant me permission to return
I promise to practice those lessons I have learned
If I fail I'll relinquish paradise so I can burn*

Pedestal

Just maybe instead of sitting around stewing,
Bringing up shit from the past about my mom,
You could focus your attention to that mirror,
And realize your pedestal's completely gone.

Dream

I Have a Dream...
That I'd eventually succeed,
Yet the weight of the cosmos
Intermittently intervene.

Mental Vacation

I don't have the patience
for that stupid meditation,
Let this Benadryl intervene
for this accelerated sedation,
It's off to la-la land
for a pleasant mental vacation,
Halt all returning flights
I'll be here for the duration.

From the Start

I'm sorry I disappointed you,

Never meant to,
Just been a fuck up from the start.

Resurrection Mary

Am I the baby of Rosemary,
I did pick up Resurrection Mary,
From the cemetery back in February,
To play Pictionary
but her company was quite dreary,
But, to the contrary,
the prescription pills did read
"Results May Vary".

This Mustn't Do

Mom, you always wiped away my tears,
In all these years, I've mourned you,
I've tried to keep your memory alive,
Mom, I'm crying as I think of you,
This mustn't do, leave these tears,
I'll wait to be comforted by you.

Linguistics

Check the ballistics,
"Yeah, I'm thinking I'm back",
Like John Wick,

Murdering linguistics.

Old Friend

Greetings Old Friend,
I apologize
I seem to have forgotten your name,
Lately I've been a bit offset
& trying to maintain,
As for you,
you look well off & basically the same,
So I bid a fond farewell
& till we meet again,
So Long Old Friend

Mom's Birthday

Hush, Hush everyone;
I reckon she'll be here any second,
As the door slowly opens in unison
everyone yells "Surprise",
The smile upon her face captures
the moment in her eyes,
A happily rejoice as she hugs
all her friends & family,
I hug her & whisper
"I love you" softly in her ear,
As her grandson grabs her face

& lovingly pulls her near,
Happy Birthday Mom,
we love you & wish you the best,
Here's too many more,
you're a God sent, we're truly blessed.

Discarded

Grown quite custom to being ostracized,
School life was no different than family life,
When you're the black sheep
love doesn't materialize,
You get discarded,
bombarded and even pulverized,
Yet my defiant integrity
will never let me compromise.

Mind Work

"While writing, how does your mind work?"
Ahem, in the deepest recesses of my mind
is where my demons lurk,
Smirking as I'm jerking off to Miley Cyrus
twerking as I go berserk,
Oh right, back to part about writing,
it's actually kind of frightening,
The sick sadistic mental images
those delightful demons are supplying,

*Peaceful tranquil memories of love kisses and
cuddlies, oh I live for these,
Kodak moments preserved so preciously,
inspiring me write love themed poetry.*

Betrayal

*Oh, I was simply distraught over her betrayal,
Until that excruciating pain of her devilish tail,
Impaled my broken heart to finale our fairytale.*

Sniper Scope

*So fucking tired of being broke,
Tired of this debt rope strangling my throat,
As these sophisticated fat cats
gloat in designer coats,
Fuck you rich pieces of shit
your life's a fucking joke,
As I catch you in the cross hairs
of my sniper scope.*

Being Ignored

*I find it difficult to
find the motivation to write,
When I rather slice a main artery
& bleed out tonight,*

Tired of being ignored,
drip blood on the keyboard,
Caption it, "I die for my art,
engulfed by the black hole in my heart".

Gobbledygook

Fuck it; I've been overlooked,
Ever since they mistook,
My poetry notebook,
For a bunch of gobbledygook,
And omitted me from the yearbook,
But you can't get rid of me
just like the Babadook.

Labeling my Heart

What are the consequences
of cutting my heart open,
Removing the love & devotion,
concocting a potion,
Eliminating emotion,
labeling my heart forever broken.

Corned Beef & Cabbage

I was born white without the privilege,
White trash Google the fucking image,

I'm Irish but fuck Corned Beef & Cabbage,
Socially below average, a bloody savage,
Intellectually astute without an Armani suit,
So being labeled inferior "Does not compute".

Just an Offshoot

Time to reboot, revert back to my roots,
Long before Russia & Trump were in cahoots,
Just an offshoot an 80's kid
mouthing off to an old coot,
Not Bernie Sanders but any teacher
that was a substitute,
Wearing a Woodsy Owl t-shirt
"Give a hoot, don't pollute!",
Drunk off that Absolut,
crashing harder than a bandicoot,
Getting my ass beat like
a Grand Theft Auto 3 prostitute.

Conjunction

"I'm afraid he's dead…"
Heart restarted from an adrenaline injection,
Back with more tenacity
then Conjunction Junction,
Binging on Coke fucking Strawberry Shortcake
With a VIAGRA® erection,

Mother fuckers I'm saying pay attention,
I'm back like 80's nostalgia
from binge watching Stranger Things,
They say, "It ain't over
'til the fat lady sings",
So I got Roseanne Barr doped up on smack
on Star Search prompting her fat ass
to sing Roxanne by Sting.

Universe

Your celestial body adorned
the magnificent universe,
While I was set adrift
in the wake of your cosmic dust.

Quite Sad

Against any reservations I may have had,
I told my Grandfather
he was more of a Father to me than my Dad,
Which is quite sad.

Tiny Parasites

Love is a fatal disease,
Contracted from a glance,
Tiny parasites devouring your heart,

No cure except…

Story Weaver

My permanent residence
still remains utter obscurity,
I vindicated my existence
through my blatant poetry,
Notably my persistence
translates to fucking obscenities,
Censoring my profanities devoids their functionalities,
Split personalities, I'm a story weaver addicted to tragedies.

Futile Attempt

Death separated you from me,
And this is all a futile attempt to
Immortalize you through poetry.

Audience to Applaud

As years passed I perfected
my pleasant little façade,
Smile & nod and wait for
the audience to applaud,
I'm not unique or odd,

I'm simply normal not flawed.

Two Redwing Dragons

Imagine being attacked by
two redwing dragons chasing me
in my Radio Flyer red wagon,
oh how nerve-racking
but Hey I'm not bragging.

Archimedes

Dammit Archimedes,
this Mountain Dew addiction
is gonna give me diabetes,
And I hate eating Wheaties
while wearing pajamas with the feeties,
And when the fuck is Adele going to
flash those big ol' floppy titties.

Splattered

My tattered hearts' been battered,
Mashed and then fucking splattered,
Completely fucking shattered,
As if its existence never fucking mattered.

21st Century

Fuck the sobriety and clean life
I'm stressed out from the constant anxiety,
Of whether or not I'll ever obtain that fucking title of "Greatest Poet of the 21st Century".

Grade School Teacher

I'd like to back hand my grade school teacher,
fuck you bitch, how the fuck did I believe her,
bullshit when I grow up
Imma be whatever I wanna be,
bitch didn't tell me
I'd be bagging her fucking groceries.

Poison

It was the consistency
It was the potency
Your selfish tendency
to Poison me constantly...
Humiliate Me, Ridicule Me,
Degrade Me, Insult Me,
With your Poison that I Gradually...
Grown immune to, Grown accustomed to,
My daily digestion of
your Spiteful Poison.

Monster

Mentally subdued is a volatile monster,
A zany cockamamie prankster,
Loud mouth millennial,
reduced to a minimal,
Suffocating screams of FUCK,
in order to NOT push my LUCK,
to NOT offend when I'm offensive,
to be modest when I'm impulsive,
Formulating methods of revenge,
Off the hinge, dastardly mind binge,
To a vegetative state,
canvas is a blank slate,
Love Trumps Hate,
as I visualize my suicide,
televised world wide,
to witness the Monster Deep Inside.

Narcissistic

I'm a Chicago native,
Polarized as slightly creative,
Narcissistic satirical poet,
Underrated yet
concertedly innovative.

Secret Crush

A socially awkward nerd
in the back of the 3rd row,
7th grade flunky being bullied
getting hit by an elbow,
Dwelling on the humility of being
depantsed in P.E.,
Surprisingly find a typed messaged
addressed to me,
A secret crush immediately
entices and ensues a crisis,
Playing right into the deception
since I'm starved for attention,
The 2nd note implies
I was being deceived and strung along,
3 simple minded freaks maliciously laugh
at me for being dead wrong.

Yo Mamma

Laugh it up with those "Yo Mamma Jokes",
As I crush your trachea strangling your throat.

Art 101

I could paint the sky with water colors,
Landscape the mountain ranges with charcoal,

Use pastel blue and green for the rivers,
Sculpt a brick house in a photographic meadow,
Finger paint a oak tree with a Popsicle swing,
Then finally sketch us in an antique art piece,
An image immortalized in my lost poetry.

I'm Free

I find myself on the edge of oblivion,
as I take a final sip of whiskey
from my dented flask.
Humming a carefree tone from my youth,
I strike a match and
light a Lucky Strike cigarette.
Tucked under my chin is a raggedy green bandana,
I tug it over my eyes as I blow out the smoke
through my nostrils into the
wind pushing against my back.
I take one final step with my black Converses
and silently plunge head first
into the dark cold abyss.
I recite repeatedly in my mind "I'm free".

Little Grouch

There's a Super Big Gulp cup
filled to the brim with
Carlo Rossi wine from a gallon bottle,

*and I guarantee
it'll be empty by tomorrow.
I stand silent wishing
I was completely invisible,
why are you drinking Mom?
Life can't be that miserable.
I only see you like every other weekend,
but once again I'm getting dropped off
to be watched by one of your
so-called friends.
Please, you can't be leaving me here…
what did I do wrong?
You left me here,
in this house with cat crap in their tub,
bed sheets draping door frames,
and strangers that smell like crud.
Eventually you return stumbling,
mumbling as some dude helps you to the couch.
"Can we go home now Mom?"
Just a blank stare as I'm pushed aside
like trash, a little grouch.
"Mom, are you okay?" She's just fine kiddo;
now go outside and play.*

5 Day Place

*Be weary of the consequences of being five,
Like telling the neighbor to kiss your ass,*

that wouldn't jive,
Especially during a custody battle
it's like swarms to the hive,
Some sick twisted lawyer
could implicate you're being abused,
Indicate a scapegoat your favorite uncle
for the accused,
Confiscate all your child bubble bath videos
to tighten the screws,
Then it's off for observation
in the hospital which in ensues,
They seem to misconstrue
my other uncle that was boozed,
That left me with a concussion,
a big bruise and that abuse wasn't used,
Thus begins the evaluations,
limited parental visitations,
Monitored playtime and extensive isolation,
For five days the conclusion,
no abuse, zilch, nada,
Just an abandonment issue for that
false yada, yada, yada.

Keyboard

I will continue to type away
until my finger tips are bloody,
And each letter on my keyboard

has subsequently broken off,
If my writing is the only way
to keep your memory alive.

Enchanting Princess

Ode to an enchanting princess,
that captured the heart of a foolish jester,
in a love trance from her hypnotizing glance,
low & behold she bestowed a miraculous smile,
upon me as I jumbled my words in her presence,
I readily confessed my endearment,
I adore you princess &
'tis my heart I impart to you.

Boombox

I want to serenade you with a Boombox
outside your bedroom window,
Playing Unforgettable by Nat King Cole
from my cassette tape radio,
"I'm wearing you down, baby"
like Steve Urkel & Laura Winslow,
We can slow dance in the back of my El Camino
just a subtle innuendo.

Non-Suicidal

Untightening this noose
& stepping down from the chair,
Becoming self aware of all those that care,
Realizing it's an unfair burden
for them to bear.

Hell's Flames

As I toss each photo one by one
into the flames,
I'm eradicating your existence
in history I'm afraid,
Maybe the only way I can see you
burning in hell,
Purging all my suffering
in this alleviating farewell.

Mercy Kill

Still I'd prefer a mercy kill,
A jagged little pill,
Exorcise the last of my dying free will.

Old Style

My city is a cesspool of depravity,

*Devoid of morality, toxicities suffocating me,
Ciudad Del Diablo better known as Chicago,
The broken concrete secretes deceit,
Corruption blatantly indiscreet
as politicians greet,
Nothing is practical in this murder capital,
Bullets for slaying children
narrated by a perverse reverend,
Remembering city pride as a juvenile,
Turning into stomach vile,
Up heaving like a 6 pack of Old Style.*

Bottled Up Future

*If I could bottle up the future,
My broken dreams & a voucher,
An insecure poet copying insincere lines
from a Google browser,
The doomsday announcer passed out
from a bottle of downers,
The world would be better off if I was
Broke on a corner selling flowers.*

Storytelling 101

*My poetry is infused with self deprecating
storytelling after being boozed,
So I refuse to succumb to depression isolating*

myself and feeling numb,
Release my thumb off the self destruct button and show off a little something,
You're about to witness the hipness of witless persistence of scaring you shitless,
My minds off kilter, my mouth no filter, helter-skelter, Say My Name like Walter White,
So I write until my memories are completely wiped.

Doomed

Darling, we were doomed from the start,
If only the past didn't sabotage my heart.

Trust Fund Babies

I wasn't born with the silver spoon prestige,
More like the alcoholic heroin spoon disease,
A lowly peasant destine to never obtain royalty,
My parents weren't rich executives,
They had to rely on the kindness of relatives,
I had no nanny only my granny to take care of me,
So fuck all you trust fund yuppie pampered babies,
I'm a rabid mongrel mutt suffering from rabies.

Plastic Bin

Here's a plastic bin,

To put your sorry excuses in,
I'll sort through them whenever
I give a fuck again.

Buried in Me

These dreams are torturing me,
Digging up the past buried in me,
Wake up & I resist the urge to cry,
The silent depression becomes amplified.

Chandelier

I wish you could've seen how sincere
my love is as a pushed you clear
of a falling chandelier, my dear.

Defiant as Hell

I've always been fucking defiant as hell,
Fuck school & took a sick day
to watch Saved by the Bell,
1st concert could've been
TMNT's Coming Out of Their Shells,
But my Prick Dad put the kibosh on that as well,
So I rebelled with the baggy pants
and blonde spiky hair gelled,
Idolizing future has-been Rock Stars on TRL,

And Fuck AOL and your bullshit You've Got Mail.

Wordsmith

I've been cursed with
being possessed by a demonic wordsmith,
A nerd with the mind of an alcoholic magician,
a homicidal mortician
& a dyslexic mathematician,
as I envisioned my word precision
could sever your head
like a head on collision.

Cookie Crook

Ever since a toddler I was a cookie crook,
If I got caught I'd give that cutsie wootsie look,
As a teen my coolness turned to gobbledygook,
A nerdasaurus without
any signatures in my yearbook.

Unicorn

Dress up as a dancing Unicorn at Comic-Con,
Reading excerpts from the Necronomicon,
Spellbound a crowd of virgins to sacrifice,
Satan, I hope these cosplayers will suffice.

My Flaws

So before all the oos and awes pause,
I need to know if you'll accept me
with all my flaws,
Help me heal as I'm wrapped in bandages
spitting out bloody gauze.

Mannequins

An unruly outcast up to more
outlandish shenanigans,
Unkempt hair karate chopping
Abercrombie mannequins,
"Ach, Ach-choo!"
Fuck you Claritin & all these
fucking allergens.

Half Deformed

I manifest in shadow form half deformed
and watch you selfishly perform,
Fake smiles in your vanity mirror for selfies
for updating your profiles,
Hiding the ugly hostile monster
underneath your bed until I manifest again,
The unrelenting demon in your head
you should've starved instead of feed.

Chainsaw Massacre

*I'm gassing up my rusty
fucking chainsaw
for a massacre,
I'm classical time traveler
with an obscene fucking vernacular,
A disgruntled millennial promised
fame & fortune but piss poor,
A recovering nonconformist
with delusions of fucking grandeur.*

Failed Poet Society

*A botched surgical lobotomy,
Locked away in solitary
in a dilapidated mortuary,
Awaiting the clumsy doctor
to perform an autopsy,
Toe tag reads inductee
into the Failed Poet Society.*

Fatherly Advice

*In the off chance I'm not here
to give you fatherly advice,
To have the talk with my sons
I'll write this down precise,*

*As a teenager love could be absolute paradise,
Or as detrimental as a nuclear device,
And some girl's egos are simply overpriced,
Let me be concise if she's intoxicated
and trying to entice,
Think twice and tell her it's been a real slice,
If she cheats on you she's not worth it
it's her loss and sacrifice,
Never do anything in anger or out
of spite always be Mr. Nice,
Never date her friends or
your friends' ex-girlfriends
that's cold as ice,
If she breaks your heart
tell your mommy
she'll give you her advice.*

Obscene Entity

*In all actuality,
I'm just an obscene entity that's about to be
uploaded to your cerebellum through telepathy,
along with misery which is
downloadable content you get for free,
since my poetry now demands a
mother fucking parental advisory.*

35

I'm practically on the verge of turning 35,
Back peddle to 18 when I thought of suicide,
What if I had died,
& the light faded from my eyes,
That thought just made me about to cry,
How fucking selfish was I,
To obsess about wanting to die.

Wallpaper

Just before I douse
the wallpaper in this old house,
And burn the past
as I watch while tears roll out,
Good-bye family memories that I'll cherish now,
My childhood home burns down as I move out.

Love Dope

They call me a Love Dope,
Struck by Cupid without an antidote,
Heart sprouted wings in the clouds it floats,
I've doodle it in all these poems I've wrote,
Toot, toot, let's sail off in my love boat.

Proud of You

Son, All I want is for you to
have everything that I didn't have as a kid,
Especially a Father that would love you
& be proud of the things you did.

Dullard

Peeled off that obnoxious Parental Disclaimer,
Am I a bit tamer or become that much lamer,
Stop interjecting myself
into these repeating lines,
Remove my identity
don't read between these lines,
Who am I self promoting myself
becoming sensitized,
Just a dullard smothered
in colored junk cluttered,
Inside and outside I hide
in a multi universe immersed,
While my self worth has been
overwhelming dispersed.

Can't Write

I'm dumbfounded tonight,
Pressing keys, I can't write,

*Nothing is coming across right,
Perfect metaphor for my life.*

Vintage 80's

*I'm vintage 80's classic,
8-bit Karate Kid tournament,
Michelangelo doing a kick flip,
And grinding on Shredder's helmet,
Gay or Not He-Man was the fucking shit,
And I still think Phoebe Cates
was the hottest 80's chick.*

Confined to a Cell

*I bid you all a fond farewell,
As my poetry flourished in hell,
No demons left to expel,
No more stories left to tell,
No book packaged up to sell,
I'm just a malevolent devil confined to a cell.*

Phantom

*Hospital bloody bandages,
Crucified by savages,
With no life advantages,
Buried like avalanches,*

Spasms like drunken tantrums,
Excuse me Madam I'm only a lowly phantom.

Invite Me In

Cold chill of autumn's crisp air
As I swing on the only remaining pair
Of swings

In the rear of a dilapidated house
I use to call my home
Even the window shutters seem to moan

A silhouette of the past is cast
Upon the porch from an open door
Inviting me in but what for?

Having to Pretend

Fuck it; I never had any friends,
only this fucking pad and pen,
I've yearned for acceptance
and popularity but until then,
I'll be plagued by self doubt
'cause I can't fucking comprehend,
Why I'm alone in a crowd and there isn't
even one person I can befriend,
And it's fucking pathetic

that I have to pretend
that I have a girlfriend.

Guillotine

Since the tender age sixteen
I've been obscene,
Tossed out a rotten tangerine
and my kid cuisine,
Let the marijuana conveniently
intervene becoming mean,
A scrawny string bean spewing words
more ferocious than a guillotine.

Nu Metal

My fucking anxieties would
never let me settle,
My intro to the Devil was Nu Metal,
Upping the ante to the very next level,
Writing out lyrics with a broken pencil,
I'm pouring my heart out
nothing fucking sentimental,
And it was essential in preventing me
from going mental.

Dumped

Crumpled poems litter my desk;
fuck I'm in a slump,
Just like a teenager's world ends
after he's dumped,
& it's pointless to talk me
off the ledge after I jumped.

Pain in my Tummy

The light flickers on the candle at your vigil,
I'm miserable;
these past 20 years have been unreasonable,
A misdiagnosis, quite ferocious,
congestive heart failure,
You're memory becoming obscure,
I tried to reassure myself
as I matured of what I've endured,
I lost my Mommy,
no relief from this pain in my tummy,
The hole in my heart,
my entire world crumbling apart,
This October 28th,
it's as if I procrastinate to orchestrate,
A poem that will never culminate
the pain inside that will never subside.

DEFCON 3

I'm an introvert in a "I recycle" T-shirt,
We're at DEFCON 3, alert Captain Kirk,
Pee-wee Herman's a pervert,
his eyes won't avert,
Madonna's cleavage
at a Def Leppard concert.

Motivation to Write

I find it difficult to find
the motivation to write,
When I rather slice a main artery
& bleed out tonight,
Tired of being ignored,
drip blood on the keyboard,
Caption it, "I die for my art,
engulfed by the black hole in my heart".

Diagnosed with GERD

I'm an absurd nerd diagnosed with GERD,
Talk about word vomit,
I'm vomiting up curse words,
While flipping the bird
just incase my speech is slurred.

Fucking Black Sheep

I'm the fucking black sheep of the family,
Go on, abandon me,
Better yet just fucking omit me,
And you fucking hypocrites,
Do your damnedest to judge me,
And my mother you shunned her,
But in her passing, oh how you loved her,
So with that guilt,
Continue to cry under your cover,
I hope that you never fucking recover.

Sad Cliché

Greetings, it's the holidays,
Safe to say, a depressive day,
Feeling alone, world turned grey,
Family's gone away, a sad cliché.

Harmonious

The harmonious struggle of an artiste
to make a perfect masterpiece,
A creativity peak siphoned out
by self doubt "You're just another
failed artiste to say the least".

Spoon Feed Antibiotics

I grew up sick spoon feed antibiotics,
With a mother addicted to narcotics,
Ejected cassettes of Hooked on Phonics,
To doodle characters from X-Men comics.

Cry On

Death inadvertently lent me
a shoulder to cry on,
"Sorry my dear boy,
your mother has passed on",
He began to weep from his empty eye sockets,
"I'll reunite you both one day,
of that I promise".

Created You

The very person that created you,
I hated you sometimes more than I loved you,
I couldn't even say good-bye to you,
Publically deny you; I was ashamed of you,
I never wanted to become like you,
Yet I miss you; regret things I said to you,
I forgive you, and want to say I love you,
Mom life hasn't been the same without you.

Sign

*She laughed rather casually at the
homeless man with the sign,
From the comfort of her
expensive automobile ride,
And as her party carefree
addictions allowed drugs inside,
She too eventually become
homeless but alas with a sigh,
The irony is wasted as she now
mimics the man begging with a sign.*

Clock

*Anxiety from the deafening of a ticking clock,
Bright white screen empty from writer's block.*

Lonely Clown

*As I smear white make up
Across my sweaty brow,
Adorning this bulbous attire,
And dance for a filthy crowd,
I parade a pompous smile,
No ovation for a lonely clown.*

Queen

As I drowned in a sea of unpleasantry,
I slowly sip English tea with royalty,
Tisk tisk the beady eyed Queen insists,
She's regretted that
soon I'll be beheaded,
Insulting her dentures
means no more adventures.

Blockhead

Sitting in class in a constant state of dread,
Face a bit red, nervous about mispronouncing the words to be read,
"Jim read the next paragraph"
is that what she said,
Wishing I hadn't got out of bed,
Even Charlie Brown wasn't this
big of a blockhead.

The Heretic

Am I a heretic
for spouting off blasphemous rhetoric,
Or am I just arrogant,
a surrogate for your merriment,
Or is this my testament,

that I am completely irrelevant.

Insane Asylum

I'm shacked & restrained in a insane asylum,
This sadist portly orderly smiles maliciously,
Electroshock therapy daily
& excruciating beatings nightly,
The surly devilish Power of Attorney assures me,
Death awaits me this very morning early.

Nuttiness

My psychologist gets so fucking pissed,
My nuttiness reciting swears at randomness,
A ventriloquist with a lack of attentiveness,
"His mouth is moving"
with bandages on his appendages,
Overdosing on sedatives & kinky fucking fetishes,
So many medicines, I'm vomiting up on ottomans,
And my closest friends are Siamese twins,
Attending AA because one's a drunk
& the other's sponsoring.

Fail to Remember

I fail to remember,
Songs we sung together,

I thought we had forever,
Mother, I am trying to remember.

Retarded

I'm the stereotypical backpack kid,
Roaming the streets is what I did,
Pocket full of heartache from being discarded,
Constantly bombarded with insults
like "are you fucking retarded",
Yet I outsmarted these ignoramuses,
these fucking suit and tie conformists,
Middle fingers up behind a censor bar from this
rebellious pacifist anarchist.

JNCO Jeans

Is it 90's retro enough for me to
wear JNCO Jeans again?
No runny nose thanks to Pseudoephedrine,
and by the way,
What the fuck is Fortnite,
I grew up with a Lite-Brite,
Cutting off rattails in preschool
like an angry little shite,
Fuck it; I'm a fucking Millennial
in my dirty mid-thirties,
STD clean despite both parents

*sharing Pina Colada slurpees
& contracting Herpes.*

MMMBop Cassette

*Found my broken cassette,
Of MMMBop underneath an old pack of cigarettes,
Memories of teenage angst without any regrets,
When AOL was my gateway to the internet,
Bryan, Lee & Speck were the
best friends I ever met,
A friendship immortalized
in the static of old VHS cassettes.*

Frosty Cold Beverage

*Is that a brain freeze
from a frosty cold beverage,
Or a brain hemorrhage,
Either way the Devil has leverage.*

Male Shawl

*Unfortunately I'm just a lost 'cause,
A discombobulated numskull suffering
from Adderall withdrawal,
A chain smoker with
empty packs of Camel menthol,*

& my beard oddly smells of alcohol,
& vomit magically appeared
on my fashionable male shawl,
While protesting high cholesterol
at City Hall yelling out, "Fuck 'em all'.

Coinkydink

Never a fan of Tiddlywink,
but what a coinkydink,
*Just found my No Strings Attached CD of *NSYNC,*
So There You Go P!nk,
two in & one in the stink,
'Cause I'm an H-Bomb like an Hpnotiq®
& a Red Bull® drink.

Showbiz

Fuck you Hollywood & Showbiz
for trying to emasculate me,
Fuck your skinny jeans,
Selena Gomez & her dyed pussy,
Intoxicated off of Starbucks mocha lattes
in Wonder Woman panties,
Stage diving into a feminist crowd
with Kate Perry supporting Hillary.

Trials & Tribulations

Administer these sedatives
for a further evaluation,
Fuck these hallucinations
& their mental augmentations,
These trials & tribulations,
"I'm crazy" in quotations.

Shower

In the beginning my little seductress
Paraded around in a skimpy towel,
To join her in the steamy shower
So I took off my cape and cowl.

Buckaroo Banzai

Fuck the Good, the Bad & the Ugly,
I'm Buckaroo Banzai battling King Ghidorah,
And Fuck Gamora,
Barbarella was the Queen of the Galaxy,
Such a fucking travesty.

Empty Inkwell

Black finger smudges on an empty inkwell,
Creativity's dried up so I bid you farewell,

A silhouette sighing as the dim light fades,
Memories evaporating as dementia invades.

Colossal Disappointment

Dear Mom & Dad,
I feel like a colossal disappointment,
I've been consumed by depression,
Writing use to relieve some of it,
But I just feel completely lost,
The façade of smiles hides it,
Clever jokes and I honestly try,
To make everyone else's life happy,
But I can't… I can't make mine.

Health

It could be detrimental to your health,
Trying to pen the pain yourself.

Lurking in the Closet

Demons lurking in the closet,
imagination making a composite,
Of a presence demonic,
shrink said I've become nyctophobic,
Crucifix nailed to my bedroom wall,
using holy water and all,

*Hoping it stops the unclear whispering
of the shadowy disfigured figure.*

Stan Lee

*No excuse me or pardon me,
My pregnant wife almost knocked over
the comic book legend Stan Lee,
At Comic Con a few months
before my 1st son's delivery,
In line for his autograph
after paying the signage fee,
Didn't expect to literally
almost run into him,
guess that was free.*

Neurosurgeon

*I hereby authorize the whiskey bourbon
burping neurosurgeon to perform
a craniotomy cauterizing the
traumatizing memories so I can make
a break through in therapy.*

Doodad

*Don't make the chicken scratch
on my notepad mad,*

I'll flip out and smash and grab
any doodad just like my Dad,
Growing up anger was the only
fucking weapon I had,
So don't chalk it up as
another obnoxious teenage fad.

Zero Empathy

What's this stench of Death
radiating off my breath,
Heart palpitating,
hemorrhaging in my chest,
resulting in cardiac arrest,
Your intoxicating lipstick
no resistance to a
charismatic hypnotist,
Your love is killing me
while smiling sadistically
with zero empathy.

Something Seems Amiss

Something seems amiss
about my penmanship it has no censorship,
My poetry and I have an abusive relationship.

WABAC Machine

*I'd commandeered the WABAC Machine,
If I could travel back to 2000
when I was an obscene teen,
Where playing Tony Hawk's Pro Skater
as Wolverine was routine,
We'd convene at your house
watching MTV with Tom Green,
Serenading the neighbors for the umpteen time
amped up on caffeine,
Between me and you I thought we were
an inseparable team,
Until I start to demean you,
driving our friendship off of a ravine,
Wish I could douse all those
bad memories in gasoline,
Let you strike a match
and burn them all to smithereens.*

Terminated

*I defied you, why was I ever created,
Only to be fucking hated and isolated,
I prayed to you to the point of being nauseated,
I tried being good but it was unappreciated,
You took my Mom leaving me devastated,
I contemplated suicide*

to the point of being infatuated,
With Death like I was intoxicated,
God why did you have to leave us separated,
Sometimes I wish my birth had been fucking terminated.

Little Euphemisms

Fuck the clever little euphemisms,
call it for what it is fucking alcoholism,
So fuck your reluctant skepticism
from a bunch of whinny adults with narcissism,
But I applaud your feeble attempt at passive aggressive criticism,
Deal with your own fucking demons it's called a fucking exorcism.

Wordsmith's Mastery

They say,
"Don't judge a book by its cover",
I snapped the spine & left
the pre-face smothered,
Even dedicated a chapter
to how death severed life with my mother,
In vulgar audacity, a wordsmith's mastery,
A disobedient deviant,
four eyed nerd miscreant,

Abandonment at the start of it,
Depression at the heart of it,
A novelty item not found on a shelf,
A fucked up life story about
how I murdered myself.

Broke Pencil

For fuck's sakes I just broke a pencil
off in my ear trying to erase
you from my brain,
And all I managed to do was lodge it
in my membrane and look like an asshole
that's insane.

Rebellious Nature

Goodbye to my rebellious nature,
Have I conformed, I'm not sure,
Under the suit & tie something refuses to die,
A word mumbles under my breath
when it use to be said aloud,
I'd unapologetically yell out
"Fuck You" but now I joined the crowd,
No Mohawk, no hair dye,
no offensive t-shirts just adulthood's routine,
Responsibility poisoned
the rebellious side of me,

Trapped inside my own mind screaming out...
"Somebody Fucking Save Me!!!"

Wondrous World

Humming the tone of a baby lullaby,
My 2nd son Terry I can't wait to hold you I
want to tell you we love you so very much,
And not only in Mommy tummy
but in our hearts you've grown,
Your big brother Damian,
Mommy & me can't wait to see you,
Our precious little baby,
a wondrous world is ready to greet you.

Gone Home

I know God has called you home,
to roam the wild fields of heaven,
to retrieve all your buried bones,
to sniff and smell the fresh wilderness air,
to bark at animals from everywhere,
but I'll miss our pleasant walks,
my little puppy's gone but not lost,
you'll always be in my heart,
'til we meet again
and you can greet me with a bark.

4 Foot Tall

*I remember from way back when,
I stood 4 foot tall just taking it all in,
every Christmas present you got me
made my head spin,
spent the whole week waiting for that weekend,
I remember from way back then,
so proud of my mother for graduating nursing,
my mother was the greatest even in passing,
You'll never be forgotten as long as
I hold this pen,
I sit with the porch light just fading,
waiting for you to come home to make me din,
always told me to keep up my chin,
walk forward never giving in,
and I still remember all
this from way back then.*

Modest

*Fuck obtaining knowledge
when I first went to college,
I wanted to be the class clown
and to be acknowledged,
My classmates came off rather snobbish
if I'm just being honest,
Lack of funds in my wallet*

as if I was impoverish,
To this conceited cloddish goddess
and I'm just being modest.

Bloody Knuckles

I wake up angry, No excuses from me,
The devils in me, Fear what's within me,
A thousand needles penetrating my heart,
Sliced up into pieces, it breaks apart,
Hallow ground erupts underneath me,
Hell's demons finally coming to get me,
I strap a cross across my knuckles,
Begin bashing heads while the devil chuckles,
"It's useless to resist, you're on my list,
Arguing with those broken bloody fists,
Life's over, face facts,
you will not be missed"

Alcohol in Hell

I wonder if they serve alcohol in hell,
Do tell prince of Darkness
the analysis didn't go well.

Divine God

Titillated after being

*exonerated after hours of
being interrogated I'm now obligated to,
Deliberate with my alter egos
I'm a schizo scarecrow
residing in limbo with a nympho,
Family abandonment shackled in a basement
for treatment of my cerebral cortex,
CAT scan of my brain reveals a vortex
disrupted at the nexus of reason and rhyme,
Delusional divine god that's battling male
chauvinist swine to start loving the vagin,
A colossal disappointment out of
pain reliever ointment
missing my Dr. Kevorkian appointment.*

Chicago Native

*I'm a Chicago native,
Polarized as slightly creative,
Narcissistic satirical poet,
Underrated yet
concertedly innovative.*

Unbalanced Washing Machine

*Fucking pathetic drug addict
when ya gonna get clean,
So unbalanced you're*

like a fucking washing machine.

Nightmare

It's like an endless night without a dawn,
It's like a nightmare you passing on,
I was praying that the news was wrong,
Keeps racing though my mind like a triathlon.

Isolation

Lord knows I've tried,
even tried to force myself to cry,
I've isolating myself ever since you died,
My world shattered to pieces,
Even mourned for you but
just couldn't say good bye,
I've watched the family fall apart
right before my eyes,
Some took you for granted
and didn't even realize,
I tried to hold onto every memory,
but now you're my shining star
up in the night sky.

Resurfaced

All the torment & pain that I locked away,

Resurfaced today, the anguish & shame,
Feelings of being betrayed since you've gone away.

Empty Martinis

What's in your head Abercrombie zombie,
Cranberries, empty Martinis
& a revealing bikini,
I'm an envy green meanie
wearing a Zumiez beanie,
Spray painting graffiti
of a Robin Williams' Genie.

#MeToo

Was that a 6.5 on the seismograph?
Or the fucking aftermath of a blood bath,
In the hallway of a 3 story building,
Bloody fist wielding, damn near almost killing,
Blood even sprayed on the ceiling,
But a gut wrenching relieving feeling,
Beating the guy stalking and assaulting my mom,
Her father napalmed him like Vietnam,
Glimpses into the moment Hiroshima
met up with an atomic bomb.

Soap Operas

Let me tell you about my Grandma B,
Drinking Caffeine Free Pepsi,
Watching Soap Operas on a 45 inch TV,
Eating Tootsie Rolls & Doritos,
Beehive hairdo,
loving Steven Seagal Kung Fu,
Biggest fan of Michael Jordon
& the Chicago Bulls,
With handfuls of pots
& pans to clap on New Year's Eve,
And yes indeed,
she bought me He-Man toys
every Friday as a kid,
An avid reader of Tabloids
& smoker of KOOL cigarettes,
No regrets, playing Bingo
with her besties & her sister,
I miss her, & her colorful barrage
of 4 letter swear words,
Flipping the bird, the coolest Grandma,
take it from this nerd,
And thank you for inspiring me to
express myself though poetry.

Camouflage Retainer

I'm an open book but I come with a disclaimer,
A smart mouth with a camouflage retainer,
Childish antics of a talentless entertainer,
It's a no-brainer,
I'm just another indecisive writer.

Sugar Tits

Got some cavities
from sucking on your sugar tits,
A misfit with a culprit princess
transmitting
over a love line,
Press rewind on my cassette mix tape
with a sticker of a heart shape,
Between your legs paradise awaits,
wrapped around your finger with no escape.

Area 51

I look like a vagrant homeless man
living in fucking shanties,
I support feminist activists
while trying to sniff their panties,
AOC is handing out my dick bronzed
as participation trophies,

As we raid Area 51 to free
all those cutsie wootsie Furbies.

More Brains

Wish I had more brains, but I born ignorant,
Just an insignificant smart mouth brat,
Getting beat with a plastic baseball bat,
But fuck all that,
I dreamt of raising above all that,
So fucking heated I could break a thermostat,
Going tit for tat like a little sociopath,
Pardon me Doc, is this the diagnosis
you've been trying to get at.

Freakazoid

I'm an unemployed Freakazoid
posing for a Polaroid,
On the psychiatric chair of an android
Sigmund Freud, Completely fucking paranoid,
that some humanoid destroyed my
high score in Asteroids.

Circumvent

All I have left is regret
that I can't circumvent,

*never expressed how much you meant
until after your Death.*

Composition Notebook

*Over 20 years of writings in
a Composition Notebook,
Long before the "likes" of you,
Instagram & Facebook,
Penning my insecurities,
pain & depressive outlook,
Trying to keep my sanity
while dealing with a tragedy,
Black sheep of the family
such a fucking travesty,
'Cause there's no mental clarity
When the Whiskey bottle's empty.*

Hot Topic

*Fucking weird, there's grey hairs in my beard,
Middle-age appeared, my coolness disappeared,
Use to shop at Hot Topic, now it's JC Penney's,
And I did all my drinking back in my Twenties,
Married with two kiddies just like the Bundy's,
Is it odd keeping this cool guy façade
while trying to rock a Dad Bod, OMG!!!*

My Jam

Fuck Taylor Swift, I'm a Avril Lavigne fan,
Like hot damn Sk8er Boi was my fucking jam Fam,
Punk Rock Mohawk with Hot Topic wristbands,
Fuckin' A middle fingers up on both hands,
Sporting the black spiked bracelets,
Kicking out the jams in a basement,
Just a nitwitted misfit
that never fucking made it.

No Spare Parts

As my world fell apart,
pain crept into my heart,
Excuse me Sweetheart,
this isn't factitious art,
It's the sort of hole in your heart so obscure
there's no spare part.

No Signs

To my family I'm nothing,
this will document the suffering,
Like the endless coloring in
the shrink's office uncovering,
Traumatizing moments to dissect
and analyze for recovering,

*Sputtering nonsense while my family
shows no signs of loving.*

Nunchuck

*Excuse the obscenities, please censor this fuck,
My mind's stuck in '99 in my red pickup truck,
Just a dumb fuck hitting myself with a nunchuck,
Awestruck that I stopped making girls upchuck,
An Irish schmuck afflicted with bad luck,
oh fuck.*

Got a Disorder

*My Dad's got a disorder,
Opposite of a hoarder,
Tossed my Mother out after
he flipped a quarter.*

Pizza Rolls

*I'm bored... bored... fucking boredom,
Look at my Facebook... fucking so dumb,
Warm up some pizza rolls... oh so yum,
Try to play Zelda... 5 mins in I'm done,
Turn on Netflix... and I chill with no-one,
Start reading It...
oh look a Boy Meets World rerun,*

Get a job loser...
fuck that I rather be a ADHD bum.

Sex Emoji

Fuck WebMD couldn't fucking
properly diagnosis me,
I acquired telepathy after your
X-ray vision zapped me,
I know exactly the kind of kinky things
you'd task me, Just text me,
but fuck there's no fucking sex Emoji,
& I'm fucking as horny as Master Roshi
at a Katy Perry and Rihanna orgy.

Bleak

My insecurities keep burrowing into me,
Like an infectious disease slowly killing me,
I'm a failure there's no point in curing me,
Ignore this and let this bleak world forget me.

Apple

Darling, it's a treacherous apple
you've plucked from the tree,
You coax me to taste it saying,
"Don't you trust me?"

Fill-in the Blank

*I'm 36 and I can't seem to put down the pen,
Heartbroken like I'm 16 again,
Grew up sick as fuck on Amoxicillin,
Hated by other kids like an 80's villain,
Parents too busy shooting up Heroin,
My mind's going blank so here's a fill-in,
You're a Fuckin' _____ .*

Daydreaming

*Grew up kicking and screaming
as my parents were leaving,
With the divorce and the scheming
I was searching for meaning,
No use in daydreaming,
was I the source or the reason,
For their hatred to deepen,
weeping as reality would creep in.*

Blotched Exorcism

*Writing was infectious,
solving mental puzzles like Tetris,
My poetry was insidious
to the world was the consensus,
Tremendous raw pain displayed*

from a kid that remained friendless,
Fuck these pretentious ignoramuses
I'm bringing awareness that
I'm the Devil's apprentice,
a wordsmith menace,
the result of a blotched exorcism
releasing an evil presence,
ostracized by these torch welding peasants.

Life of the Party

Fucking I get more excited,
than Hillary if Trump got indicted,
Life of the party
that ignited dog shit on your porch
since I wasn't invited,
Delighted at the prospect my poetry
will be recited by others
since it's not copyrighted,
With "Fuck You" highlighted.

Life Sentence

Became acquainted with a demonic presence,
In my adolescence it was almost omnipresence,
Fuck acceptance, pop a pill of antidepressant,
It became more apparent after I lost a parent,
It was inherent, product of a failed marriage,

Their hateful wreckage manifested itself
into that demonic presence,
Which attached itself to me for a life sentence.

Always Dreaded

Always dreaded the day we'd have the talk,
My four year old son asked me about my Mom,
His Grandma Kathy, so I showed him pictures,
"Where is she?" he asked,
I told him she's gone,
She passed on, she died,
and he asked "Why?,
Was it a Monster?"
No son, it was just her time,
She passed away when Daddy was little,
"Did it hurt?" Yeah Daddy was sad,
But she's always with us and we remember her,
Whenever we visit the cemetery
and bring balloons,
"Daddy, can we save her?"
No little bear,
we can't,
But just know that she loves you
very much just like we do.

Pandora's Box

I meticulously sort all my problems
into Pandora's Box,
Which is appropriately sealed
with a combination padlock,
So please take stock my poetry
isn't about the awe & shock,
The pen's a pistol that loaded
& half cocked at those that mocked,
Ridiculed & knocked, so best believe
that now you're all fucking focked.

Hate Vegetables

In grade school transitioned
from public to private school,
But I was constantly the subject of ridiculed,
Even the teachers & principle
made me feel miniscule,
This fucking cesspool of
ignorant fools labeling me un-cool,
High upon their pedestal
I was hated more than kids hate vegetables.

Apple Tree

"Oh come see, the new bright

red apple on the apple tree",
Oh how they admired that apple
until it got a bit stormy,
And broke a branch on that apple tree,
That bright red apple hung split
between the two branches until
It fell to the ground and was forgotten
by the rest of the apple tree,
There it decayed into the ground
only to grow its own apple tree.

4th Birthday

For my 4th Birthday I dressed up as Rambo
going commando and ate a She-Ra cake,
For fuck's sake Dad I look a bit effeminate,
shout out to r.m. Drake.

Text Message

Enough of the cliché love quotes,
& the romanticized exchange of love notes,
I delight at the sight of via text messages
from my Nokia cell phone.

Eternia

Just call me Skeletor,

*you can be my Evil-Lyn,
Together we'll defeat He-Man
& conquer Eternia for the win,
You bumbling boob Beast Man,
did you forget the wedding ring?
Myaah!!!*

Irish Bloke

*Fuck your commercialized poetry
mimicking clever little Mark Twain quotes,
"Her love is an ocean till you
drown in it and choke",
I nick an artery for my artistry & bleed
for what I wrote,
I'll sever my own throat with a broken whiskey
bottle like a real Irish bloke,
Your poetry is trivial &
vague like a cheap prostitute,
I applause my audience
because they seem more astute,
I'm the entire shot of bourbon
while you're just a dilute.*

BIG

*As a kid they'd tell you to dream big,
Fuck Tom Hanks I'm talking about BIG,*

*Big as King Kong
on the Empire State building BIG,
Big as Pamela Anderson's tits
on Baywatch BIG,
Big as the drug addiction
of Jim Morrison BIG,
Big as the orange buffoon
in the White House BIG.*

Serendipity

*Serendipity,
I find tranquility
in your misery.*

Hellspawn

*She was disingenuous
with her charismatic façade,
An immaculate fraud, a hellspawn,
Souvenir scars from once I was clawed.*

Shall We

*Shall we commence with
the decompression of my depression.*

Elephant

Visually, I am as insane as an elephant
snorting a Columbian cargo plane of cocaine.

Savoir

Manufactured to be a failure,
Please excuse the erratic behavior,
Consumption of narcotics
will not lead you to your savoir,
My pencil writes my life story
but death follows it with an eraser.

Death

Lull bamboo forest
Decimated samurai
Seppuku death

Greetings from Hell

Greetings, you just interrupted my demons
mistreating me with a relentless beating,
Awkward form of meeting me stung up
on the ceiling, whose scene am I stealing,
As a horde of demons demand feeding,
honestly at this point you should

probably start fleeing.

The Loss Group

*After my Mom died,
I could've self-destructed,
Luckily I was reluctant;
found something more constructive,
Instead of my mind on a constant loop,
sitting on a stoop,
School placed me in something
called "The Loss Group",
A group of teens that had
their hearts ripped apart,
where do I start,
Some found comfort in
abusing until I tried to impart,
You're tarnishing their memory,
making them your accessory,
Would they really want to be
the reason for your self-destruction,
If you're feeling lost so are we
so let's open it up for discussion.*

All Night Vigil

*An all night vigil set against
a bright crescent moon back drop,*

*Mourn the loss & treasure
the moments captured there within,
Sing praises for love & life
as we rejoice in your memories,
Warmth from the chill of night,
warmth from lit candles & smiles,
Your presence in our lives...
missed & cherished equally,
Solidified through the
irreplaceable impressions you've left,
Journey onward; seek out new ventures
within Heaven's light.*

Family Tombstones

*As I stagger amongst the graveyard
of family tombstones,
Utterly alone, unbeknown since family
has forgotten these buried bones,
My mom is here, my cousin,
uncles, grandparents
and that sobering feeling that
I must atone and pay my deepest respect
for the love that you have kindly shown.*

Why Was I Created

As I crumble away, it's painful to stay,

My entire existence screaming save me,
I never felt wanted, why was I created,
For a lifetime of crying alone, I hate me.

Out of Orbit

Death of my mom knocked my world out of orbit,
My poetry turned morbid,
the black ink wouldn't absorb it,
Wasn't long till forged alliances,
shorted out like home appliances,
In school went from pluses in sciences
to negatives and minuses,
Excuse me your royal highnesses
taking advantage of my kindnesses,
I'll blow a little snot
like you right out of my sinuses,
Started huffing and puffing
and blowing everything down,
Treating people like shit guess it
was bound to come back around,
My friends weren't having that,
abandoned me at the drop of a hat,
That anger got recycled into an endless cycle
of me giving it back,
Instead of dealing with the pain
I cut my own throat capillary vein,
So instead of soaking up the sun rays

I was drowning in the rain.

Freedom of Speech

**Yawn* droning on about
differential equations Teach,
I get a ~~fucking~~ hard on
from my Freedom of Speech,
I like sentence enhancers like,
"You're a ~~cock~~ sucking leech."
Good Lord Son, that's blasphemy
that stuff that you preach,
Sorry Padre, I'm slapping the nun's ~~ass~~
that's as sweet as a peach,
And ~~fuck~~ political correctness,
her sugar ~~tits~~ are just out of reach,
And pardon my antics; it's for the
Death of the Freedom of Speech.*

Terrible Twos

*Congratulations, I'm on my fucking way
Graduated those dastardly terrible twos
Consolation prize was getting physically abused
Overbearing Granny wasn't about the awes & woos
More like tossing a glass ashtray at my back
And leaving a hell of a bruise
Apparently she despised me hopping around*

Like a rambunctious joey kangaroo
Proceeded to clobbering me with a plastic bat
That left plenty of welts which got 0 views
Now you expect me to write her eulogy
Imagine that bullshit so fuck it I refuse.

School Bell

Tell the teacher I'll excuse myself from class,
Plotting how to defuse the school bully from attempting to whoop my ass,
Fire crackers tied to his bike wheels popping off as I methodically laugh,
I haul ass dashing back to class as fast as DC's Flash,
Wink over at the cute girl next to me thinking I'm the shit,
As she insinuates that I induce her to want to vomit,
Cupid's love comet is interrupted by the bully's grunts,
Nostrils flaring up as his knuckles engage my face,
If that's the case it must be revenge for my clever little stunt,
My nose's blood drips on the bully's shoes,
A kick to my gut leaves me breathless I believe my ass is stew,

*By now my fellow classmates
are cheering him on,
Flash backs to yesterday when
he had my head shoved
in the bathroom John,
Never been brawny brain power
for this weak and scrawny,
School bell rings class's out Bully's
walking home fuck you I ain't sorry.*

Mr. Robot

*"Please Stop!" I will not
I'm Mr. Roboto's robot.*

Cassette Tape

*I'm Breaking Bad riding around
with Gustavo in a Tahoe,
Stupid kids quoting Yolo,
Big Pun tell the kids "Maldito Pendejo".*

Coffin

*I start pounding on the lid of the coffin,
Exhausting punching till my skin softens,
Coughing oxygen depleting knuckles bleeding,
Fuck screaming and this whispering demon,*

Trying to breathe in, wielding wrist bleeding,
Scheming and feening before I face leaving,
Weakening thoughts wakening I'm taking in,
Heaven's welcoming I refuse to be giving in,
Finally I start breaking in this fucking coffin.

Excuse Me

Excuse me Padre,
but save the prayers and sermons,
Summon the sadistic lunatic devil
possessed surgeons,
Numbing the excruciating pain with some bourbon,
I'm curbing my enthusiasm
for life's unbearable burdens.

Surrender

Paradise's escape,
I float quietly in a bottle of whiskey,
Tropical's landscape,
I request bartender don't tip me,
Moonlight drapes,
I feast only from a fruitful peach tree.
Translucent state,
I digress soul surrender let this be.

Cosmic Joke

Has it become cliché to say my heart is broke,
I was so happy to be with you then I awoke,
Feeling of loss hits again like a cosmic joke.

Constant Fuck Up

"You're never good enough, a constant fuck up"
That little voice that resides inside like a
sadistic lullaby,
This fucking birthright of misery
that accompanies me,
Is it arrogance to refuse
this so called family inheritance.

Touchy Subject

As I attempt to recollect,
Whether it was the jealously or neglect,
It remains a touchy subject.

The Path

As I walked with you down the off beaten path,
We reminisced about the past
& had ourselves a laugh,
As we came upon that

metaphoric fork in the road,
Our friendship parted ways again
& cancelled our reunion episode.

White Rabbit

Intoxicated I followed the
white rabbit down the rabbit hole,
Tumbling downwards into
a imaginary nightmare of regret,
Glimpses of childhood trauma
in vivid details hallucinated,
As the white rabbit reveals herself
as a psychiatric nurse,
Perpetuating my fears and
manifesting my inner demons.

Fuck Work

Fuck work & my boss,
I'm staying home to eat some Häagen-Dazs.

Breath Away

She's so unbelievably kind,
She takes my breath away,
As she smothers me
Like the Chief did

to a lobotomized McMurphy.

Blimps

My childhood companion Teddy Ruxpin
Told nightly tales of airship blimps
And adventures I thought would last
But the magic faded
As I became oblivious
To the magic around me

Moonlight

Monsters lurking in shadows
Brought to life by Moonlight
Under the bed, In the closet
I hide under
My Ghostbusters' Bedsheet

Butterfly

We floated up a
butterfly balloon this afternoon,
At the cemetery while we were visiting you,
In celebration of your Birthday today,
And by the way, don't let me forget to say,
I love you and I will always miss you, Mom.

Yes Sir

*Yes Sir,
I'm a failure,
but failure didn't detour me from venturing
on life's quirky little adventures.*

Deceive

*I believe I was only 2
when he conceived to deceive,
Lead my mom to believe
everything was routine,
Indeed his degree of deceit
was beyond belief,
Talk about intrigue
making love before you leave,
Retrieved your belongings
and your offspring seed,
And leave your devotee wife
for your own selfish greed.*

Pulitzer Prize

*I'm a sadistic brainiac
inside sulfuric acid filled amniotic sac,
Imagine the visual for that,
my poetry deserves a Pulitzer Prize*

From those Fat Cat Aristocrats,
Sincerely yours,
a Narcissistic Fucking Spoiled Brat.

No Rhodes Scholar

Thank God that I'm a Father,
Have a preschooler & a toddler,
& their Grandfather was no Rhodes Scholar,
Just a bar room brawler, blue collar,
Working hard for every dollar,
So I wasn't raised in squalor,
I thank him & my Grandfather,
For everything that made me stronger.

Must've Been Hard

All I've ever heard was
"Must've been hard losing your mom at 14",
Imagine your mother,
your nurturer at the mercy
of an executioner under the guillotine,
Wishing to God someone
or something would intervene,
Crying unseen as this chapter
with your mother comes to its final scene.

Woodstock

Your poetry's too real, there's no mass appeal,
You're just like that black & white beagle,
Sitting on a red roof top
with a clichéd typewriter,
Dangerous as an ambitious idea igniter,
Burning your verses
with a Woodstock cigarette lighter.

Country Bumpkin

After a night of kick boxing a country bumpkin,
For wearing a "Make America Great Again" pin,
Me and my drunken friend
a Mister Freakin' Teddy Ruxpin,
Ate in at a Huck Finn's after a bit of the
ol' in-out with a sultry vixen Mary Poppins.

Error, Does Not Compute

"Error! Does Not Compute!"
I follow suit to check
the input of the amenities,
These inconsistencies in this robot's remedies,
Prolong exposure to a broken heart,
Palpitating till it explodes
and becomes abstract art,

"Error! Does Not Compute!"

0 Likes

*Still got 0 Likes for me riding
a fucking Tandem bike last Friday night
Trying to incite a pussy riot
on Skype #thatshitwastight
Even Jimmie Walker was
yelling out fucking "Dy-no-mite!"*

Raise My Kids

*My Dad decided to give me some
fatherly advice how to raise my kids,
But where the fuck where you Dad
when it came to raising this kid,
Absentee, take it from me,
a few fond memories but mostly absentee,
Whether it was your road to becoming
a divorcee or recovering druggie,
Some walks in the woods on a weekend
barely counts as properly raising me.*

Trouble Maker

*My little trouble maker is almost two,
Climbing, jumping and kicking kung fu,*

"Dada, park" sliding down the tallest slide,
Amazing all the excitement in his eyes,
"Dada, book" reading in the stormy weather,
Adventures galore as we explore them together,
"Dada, love you" and I love you too,
Goodnight my little dude, time to go choo choo.

Poster Child

I'm the legit poster child
for the druggie's fucking 80's,
Two druggie parents
spawning a little hell of Hades,
Sprinkled angel dust on
the baby mobile above my crib,
Injecting heroin leaving
old apricot sauce on my bib,
A custody battle feuding
like the rivals in Lucky # Slevin,
That judge said "I rather send
this child back up to heaven."
Greylord Scandal made that
same judge put a gun to his head,
Held his purple heart and
blew his brains all over a tanning bed.

Selfish Vices

Sobering up from these selfish vices,
A loathing that'll entice us,
To the lumber through nostalgia
During a quaint little mid-life crisis.

Snack Pack

I shutter at the cold wind blowing at my back,
The Ninja Turtle backpack
packed like a pack rat,
School bus packed us in no room in the back,
So I sat next to a fat kid
scarfing down a snack pack.

Bridges

Typically they advise
"Don't burn your Bridges",
But I've never been too fond of
being shit on by Pigeons,
Douse them in gasoline
& incinerate them to ashes,
Cross me is like summoning
a horde of Gremlins,
Praying in churches as
I blow off the door hinges,

Resurrect witches to burn stakes
of faithless Christians,
Witness glimpses of hoaxes,
boos and childish hisses,
As squadrons of talons tear
you apart like surgeons.

Smoldering Ash

I just turned sixteen,
Come sit with me,
As I douse myself in gasoline,
Sarcastically I ask for a light,
What an eventful night,
You can witness me end my life,
And if my family bothers to ask,
Their answers lie in the smoldering ash.

Bucket List

Crumbled up my bucket list,
I'll never learn how to play guitar,
travel afar, buy a Delorean car,
be a fancy Hollywood Star,
or even own an Irish bar,
Only have the means to travel
Across country in a freight train boxcar.

Never Been Cool

Fuck I've never been cool,
Not even back in high school,
I was the subject of ridicule,
Scoffed at from your pedestal,
But at least I wasn't two-dimensional.

Late Night TV

Save your psycho babble from late night TV,
And please no more suggestive psychotherapy,
The killer clown demon in my dreams
trying to kill me,
Said I'll be dead before you can
properly diagnose me.

Inhibited by the Devil

Inhibited by the Devil or was it enabled,
My thoughts are sporadically scrambled,
Speaking with a forked tongue in rambles,
As my entire life has been left in shambles.

Can't Fix Me

There's nothing you can do to try and fix me,
I've been broken inside

since you neglected my first infant cry,
Since I skinned my knee, stung by a bee,
Got my first stitches, broke my first bone,
Broke birthday wishes, left me all alone.

Answer the Phone

An ominous tone as I answer the phone,
Dead silence accompanied by static,
Inducing mental panic, I'm frantic,
"Mom… is… that… you…?"

Cryostasis

As I prepare for suspended animation,
A hiatus as I finally enter cryostasis,
My interlude of minimum magnitude,
Cue the symphony of love and agony,
An empty apology, this may very well be,
The final time you ever hear from me.

Pity Party

*Distance myself from my heart broken
in pieces on the floor,
Expected too much from us,
just to overwhelming to ignore,
So damn easy falling into love,*

but when shit breaks bad,
Time to replace those pictures on the shelf,
Attempting to repair it
only leaves me arguing with myself,
And it feels like the world stops
before imploding on itself,
Black hole opens up without any warning,
with no fucking help,
Memories that you cling to, distract you,
bring you right back,
To the pity party you're throwing
instead of just facing facts,
Love would be the conqueror,
break up the aftermath,
Try to fit us back together,
never focused on the path,
Dragging me along kicking screaming
in the dirt,
Wish I never met you,
to save me from the hurt,
Wish I never wore my heart on the sleeve
of my shirt.

Childhood Ills

I fear the onset of dementia,
Or diagnoses of schizophrenia,
Both manifested in my familia,

I regurgitate pills as whiskey spills,
As I reignite dreadful childhood ills.

Baked

I won't even be famous
long after I'm Dead
might as well get baked
with Mr. Potato Head.

Sarah

She's magnificent in beauty
as she is in heart,
She had me wrapped around her finger
for the very start,
From Spider-Man comics to Dragon Ball Z,
From prank calling people
to being my smoking buddy,
From matching Mountain Dew shirts
& Converse shoes,
To playing video games
like Fable & Guitar Hero all afternoon,
To inspiring my ambitions
from making movies to writing poetry,
She's my motivation in life,
my gorgeous wife, the better half of me.

October 29th 1997

*Stupid assignment of
keeping a journal entry,
Rather be doodling art
for the girl next to me,
It's math class algebra
solve this mathematical equation,
X plus Y equals something of course
not paying attention,
Suddenly my name echoes out
over the school's intercom,
Report to the principle's office
relax Jim just remain calm,
Sense of deep deep trouble
as my heart rate doubles,
Imagining excuses guess that's
how the cookie crumbles,
As I enter the office
the fear finally kicks in,
As I see my dad there welcoming me in,
It's game over man as he escorts me outside,
Suddenly I'm 5 again resorting
to trying to hide,
Face down as he mutters
something I could barely hear,
Something about my mom's gone,
eyes holding back tears,*

Time ceases to exist
mind racing from being pissed,
This nightmare isn't real,
must've been something that I've missed.

Grandpa AA

Peddle faster Grandpa,
I betcha you'll never catch me,
Especially with my blue bike
with training wheels,
You'll be a slowpoke Magee,
You move as slow as snails,
Hiding between these concrete rails,
I betcha you'll never find me,
As we race around Gage Park School
I let out a loud "Yippee".

Drive faster Grandpa,
I hope we won't be too late,
I know,
I know at the Doctor's office
we always have to wait,
But today I get my braces off,
my teeth are finally straight,
Finally no bullies chasing me,
finally getting a clean slate,
And if I turn out half as cool

       as Grandpa
  Maybe I'll finally get a date.

     Knock harder Grandpa,
  Come on I'm trying to take a nap,
  Geez you visit like everyday,
  I'm playing Nintendo "Zap, Zap",
  It's off to my little league game,
    wait I forgot my lucky cap,
     Come on, speed up Grandpa,
use the accelerator not the brake tap,
   I've always been a smart mouth
   and you'd tell me to shut my yap.

       Work harder Grandpa,
   geez it's like 100 degrees out,
     Re-shingling your garage,
   Oops there goes the water spout,
   When fixing things you always been
          knowledgeable about,
       You'd never lose your cool
       never once scream or shout,
      Even when I broke the toilet
      and the water all spilled out.

         Miss you Grandpa,
  found out today that you've passed on,
    You were larger than life to me,

my very own icon,
I'm grateful for the times we had
and for our special bond,
I'll always share our stories,
that way you'll always live on,
Thank you Grandpa,
for all the love you've shown me,
Love always your Grandson.

Angry Blonde

Rest in peace to my mom,
the original angry blonde,
Delivered me that same year
as Wrath of Khan,
Right before my dad transformed
into a Decepticon.

Greed

Some place between making the payment
or getting kicked to the pavement.

Broken Sky

The sun sets on a broken sky,
The night remembers neither you nor I,
And distance is something we can't escape,

You're in heaven and I'm just misplaced,
I wander the streets lost looking for home,
The street lights shine in an ominous tone,
While darkness covers the night sky,
The night remembers neither you nor I.

World's End

They can burn the canvas
of the mural of our love,
They can even drop an atom bomb
on us from above,
Devastate the landscape
leaving nothing but a dove,
Symbolizing our undying love,
Not even Death could attempt to push or shove,
They can scorch every poem I wrote into ashes,
Bottle it up, toss it in the ocean,
it can take its chances,
Wash away our names written in the sand,
Lock us away forever in
completely different lands,
I'd still write about our love
even with broken hands,
The reality is Cupid could never produce
such a perfect couple,
Even if he was far sighted
and always shot in doubles,

I love her and she loves me
till the very end,
Nothing can break that
not even the world's end.

Out of Tune

And I'll strum this guitar
even though it's out of tune,
And sing you
the cheesiest love songs all afternoon,
And I'll promise you
that it'll always be me & you,
And I'll kiss you
& say thank God that I found you.

Winter

Winter covers up; she'll let me in,
Dying in silence, I won't fight it,
Frozen finger tips won't let me go,
She'll be mine until my heart thaws.

Hypocrite

Swirling my spoon in a bowl of Alpha-Bits,
The soggy milky letters spell out hypocrite.

Marionette

My existence is rather like
an entangled marionette,
Cordially performing
with a uncoordinated quartet,
Rhythmically twirling to
a melodious solo clarinet.

Salute

Middle finger salute to these
Bougie ass snobs,
Off my meds I'm more mischievous than
Calvin and Hobbes.

Proud Man

A proud man once walked among the giants
Standing tall with his head held high
Knowing all the pride in his heart
And with a determined spirit
That drove him to move mountains
And even impact so many lives
How do I walk in his shadow?
With the Courage to believe as he had
That one can walk among giants
And be so proud to be just a simple man.

Keep This Brief

I digress that my rebellious antics have ceased,
Diluted Whiskey because my tolerance decreased,
Not as skinny and animated but still not obese,
Censored my potty mouth like **** the police,
Grew a long beard most likely
as an artistic motif,
And I use poetry to express myself
but I'll just keep this brief.

Erase

If I could disperse with pleasantries,
Middle finger up to all my enemies,
High five all these petulant wannabes,
Erase friendships & save the memories.

Fringe

Part of the fringe
I cringe
as my beard just singed
as I inject this orange syringe
of liquid toxin into
my intestines to binge
to let my mind unhinge
and let my obscenity words infringe.

Carefree

Ever had your world turn to pandemonium,
Like Marvin the Martian with plutonium,
Space modulator on Nickelodeon,
Eyes glued to the 22 inch television set,
Drinking red barrel juice with chicken nuggets,
Thanks for the afternoon snack mom,
Carefree kid whenever DuckTales was on.

Warning Letter

Shuffling down the hall,
Back pack draped over my right shoulder,
Scribbling drawings on my school folder,
Fast forward I'm older,
Reminiscing on not paying attention,
Afternoons of after school detention,
Catching a beating,
Winding up in the principle's office
for a meeting,
Coughing and sneezing,
Walking home with a warning letter
that my dad won't be reading.

Sleepy Hallow

Formidable force pulsating through my corpse

Trampled and forgotten in reminisce of decay
Daylight starved, tired armed bursting
through dirt & clay
Resurrection of magnificent evil incarnated
A legion of demons waited
to execute the scandalized population
Hordes of strangulated deranged corpses
charged up from extension cords
Different pigments of flesh feasting
upon mankind's unrest
Hatred spewed by Satan's witches' brews
of eye ball stews
Hatred ensues as decapitated horsemen
enforce early curfews

Internal Demon

Fist punching in, connected into him,
Feeling bones cracking and being broken,
Force of impacting the numbing reacting,
Blood and fragments breaking through skin,
Fists keep punching till swelling kicks in,
Never will I win, defeated by my internal demon.

Emptiness

Stitched the word emptiness
in my pocket seams,

Amongst a button, lint & a token
from Chuck E. Cheese,
Constant reminder I'm a failed artiste,
But more followers than a Catholic Priest.

Shut In

The compulsiveness of being a shut in,
Shades drawn, Whiskey bottles filled
With Emptiness, Emphasis on being
Reluctant to socialize, to be so withdrawn
From life even my sadness is desensitized.

Cranium

Only way to remove this internal pandemonium,
Is to open up my overstuffed
complexity of a cranium,
Export the devils, demons,
obsession with death,
The insulting of
celebrities and obscenities left,
No complex rhyming,
tales of drinking and being broke,
No storytelling of loss,
just suppress the words till I choke,
No personal tragedy,
conflict or drowning out hope,

*No more lyrical content,
word play or advocating against
addition to dope,
Just write trivial sentence
fragments of simplicity,
And reference everything as love poetry
written with She,
Like she did, she said,
she is and you'll finally obtain
publicity and celebrity
for your monotony poetry.*

Slumber

*As I slumber off to bed,
counting sheep inside my head,
I dreamt of you like I said,
please don't wake me till the end.*

Dear Son

*Dear Son,
ever since I heard you were in the womb,
All 9 months leading up to that delivery room,
I assume you can hear me talking to you,
Telling you all about my day & by the way,
Your mom's amazing,
I tell her how beautiful she is every day.*

Mushy

*My heart turned
to mushy drippy goop
when I first saw you.*

Guardian Angel

*Son,
allow me to tell you about
your guardian angel,
Her name is Grandma Kathy
& she's a special angel,
Although you can't see her,
she'll always sing to you,
"You are my Sunshine"
just as she sung to me too,
Whenever you feel a gentle brush
of your hair,
Remember it's just her letting you know
she's there,
She couldn't be prouder
& she couldn't be happier,
She loves her grandson & Son,
you couldn't be luckier.*

Mom's Lullaby

Weepy eyed, heartache
You lulled me into a dream
Comforting whispers
Called me into a open field
Majestic scenery, you returned to me
Purple satin dress, beautiful angel
Soothing smile, loving embrace
"I'll always be with you"
Easing my mournful tears
I awake jubilated, Mom
Grinning from ear to ear

Crow

As I relinquish my murdered soul
For acquiring the means for revenge
I'm highly volatile in my insurrection,
The Prince of Darkness grants me redemption,
And invokes his powers for my resurrection,
"Can't rain all the time" I softly whisper,
"They're all dead" I pronounce a bit raspier,
Fortified images of our love making,
With a backdrop of thunder & lighting,
My flowering beauty permanently immersed,
In the soil ignites my hatred & turmoil,
Heaven, release me from this horrid feeling

Of being eternally forsaken & cursed.

Scattered

*Scattered amongst the debris,
Is this the life you left for me.*

Potential

*Divulge my rhyme scheme being simple,
Like a 38 snub nose against my temple,
Deprived of a conscious yet whimsical,
So cynical I sabotage myself from ever reaching the pinnacle of my potential.*

Song Bird

*Alas my Darling,
I spread tales of our romance,
Through a exquisite song bird serenading,
That you merely dismissed
as a pesky bird's chirping.*

Keepsake Box

*There's a rusty old lock on my keepsake box,
I lost that small key so it won't open for me,
All those memories inside will be lost to time,*

So I'll just store it away until my dying day.

Wonder Woman

Contemplating the tremendous strength,
Fighting drug addiction from the very brink,
Of overdosing and not sugar coating,
The truth from me, Mom you've inspired me,
When everyone abandoned and walked out,
You fought back and took the ambiguous route,
Proceeded and succeeded to follow your heart,
Became a nurse and set course for a new start,
You're the embodiment of a Wonder Woman,
And you taught me to never give up on who I am.

10/28/18

October 28th 2018
Dear Mom,
It's that time of year again,
Eyes swelling up holding it all in,
21 years since Death introduced me
to Misery as a constant companion,
I felt so abandoned,
not at all how I could have imagined,
A lifetime of graveyard visits
to leave roses in it,
I pray for your happiness

and wish you could be here to witness this,
The preciousness of your two
Grandchildren but Mom I'll tell you this,
I'll always share your memories in poetry so
possibly you'll live on for centuries,
So the world could see
how much you truly meant to me.
Sincerely,
Your loving Son, Jimmy

Dr. Seuss Fanatic

What's more fucked up than
a satanic drug addict,
Me back at it,
rhyming like a Dr. Seuss fanatic,
One needle hypodermic,
a deadly epidemic or am I allergic,
And fuck this demonic Richard Simmons
fat shaming me that
I'm not athletic or aerobic.

No Conscience

They say I tend to get a bit finicky
No conscience, No cricket like Jiminy.

Irish Banshee

*The Irish banshee dancing atop
the tombstones along the county side,
Shrieking in a gown of green
with her apple red hair brushed aside,
Alluring drunken Irishmen to court
her for a traditional Irish dance,
Revealing her true ghoulish appearance
and killing them with a glance.*

Dreamland

*As soon as those droopy eyelids close,
I'm transported back to dreamland,
Only a translucent state of consciousness,
Vivid concoction of loss and regret,
Visitation from my mother, who's passed on,
Pure anger for her abandonment of me,
Shouting over every excuse or apology,
Like she moved away and started a new life,
Without me but I wake up crying,
God why must you constantly torture me?*

Kills Me

*The malicious psychotic killer
stalking me in my dreams,*

*Racing a devilish gauntlet
as he attempts to murder me,
And he kills me, I wake up,
and I'm still in a dream
And he kills me, I wake up,
and I'm still in a dream
And he kills me, I wake up,
and I'm still in a dream
And he kills me, I wake up,
and I'm still in a dream*

Reel Life

*The reel of the projector spins an image
on a white screen.
A young couple being told they'd never conceive.
Despite a miraculous miracle of giving birth,
They divorced after 2 years
casting a dark cloud over his head.
His family scorned him,
his classmates loathed him,
He was an outcast and neglected by most.
Always seeking acceptance
but receiving rejection.
Why am I here?
I wasn't supposed to be in this existence.
Am I here to suffer in
isolation and loneliness?*

I shouldn't have been born,
I should've snuffed myself out
with my own umbilical cord.

The Pit

Rock bottom, a deep empty pit,
I sat all alone, started calling it home,
Days passed, weeks, maybe even months,
Until that fateful day I heard your voice,
I felt my spirit hoist as you
Shined a light saying "Is anyone there",
And in my despair you found me there,
Rescuing me from that egregious pit.

Hereditary

Sorry.But...
To the contrary,
Is being fucked up hereditary?

Elementary

Been an outcast since Elementary,
Failed in Chemistry,
I thought it was there but you never noticed me,
I sat behind you staring like a sentry,
Dear Journal Entry, Maybe I can captivate her with

*some poetry, "Your beauty is like a…"
Ahh... whaddaya expect from me,
Fucking wizardry make you fall in love with me,
Some things are never meant to be
like you and me.*

Construction Paper Hearts

*In Art,
I'd doodle "I Love You"
on construction paper hearts,
You'd crumple them up or rip them apart,
I wish you were sweeter my little sour tart,
'Cause when we're older you might regret
you broke my heart.*

Audience

*Usher in the audience,
cue up the crucial critical scene,
The mournful depressed boy
crying completely unseen,
In the funeral parlor as he hears
his family's screams,
At the foot of his mother's casket
like a horrible dream,
He remotely shuffles in
dragging his own two feet,*

*Foreboding the sight
of his mother adorned to greet,
Him for the final time
as he pleads God wake me,
Let her be alive instead
of this unconceivable end scene.*

Log Off

*Log off my accounts,
Shut the world out.*

If These Walls Could Talk (1)

*"If these walls could talk…"
Behind the tattered sunflower wallpaper décor,
Grew a few inches from
the summer of '86 to '94,
NES cartridges scattered amongst
the toys on the floor,
Doodles of Ninja Turtles
my uptight Granny didn't go for,
Watching the Ghostbusters V/H/S tape
that my Mama had to record,
If these walls could talk
they'd share my message like a
bottle washing up on the shore.*

Took One on the Chin

I took one on the chin
when I let her back in,
Disappointing but her lips were tempting,
Complicating our story's ending.

No Achievement Award

No achievement award
for being dead inside a morgue,
But my anger endured,
something evil had occurred.

Wuzzle

Fuck it, I was a Care Bear, she was a Wuzzle,
Two different pieces to two different puzzles,
Double the trouble means more beer that I guzzle,
The argument bubble erupts into a tussle,
My facial hair's stubble so now we can't cuddle,
A dysfunctional couple, fuck being subtle,
So I buried the past along with the shovel.

Worth Hiding

I don't feel like writing,
but it's better than self medicating and dying,

My inner demons always be lying,
so I hide my tears while I'm crying,
"Believe in yourself" trust me I'm trying,
but some pain is worth hiding.

No Thanks

I wish when I was younger,
I'd forgo the suspense and wonder,
Know the outcome before you
gave me your number, So I could say,
"No thanks I think I rather enjoy my summer".

Hash

Suffering succotash,
my hash pipe's out of hash,
Fucking hate Instagram,
I'm sitting in a pentagram,
Naked with an Ouija board,
asphyxiating from a electric cord.

If These Walls Could Talk (2)

If these walls could talk…
Sprayed with brain matter
and blood splatter left in an arch,
Behind the Mohawk kid the World ridiculed

and mocked,
Rigor mortis settling
in his hand holding a glock,
Suicidal thoughts took over
when he suffered from writer's block.

Snuggly

Living comfy & snuggly in your tummy mommy,
Smiling fetus enthralled
as you sing & talk to me,
I guarantee I'll give you unconditional love
as your baby,
And just maybe we'll be a happy family
together mommy,
But just as abruptly I felt a
suction enter the womb,
Fight or flight as my initial response
to certain doom,
Mommy I assume this is a mistake,
for an innocent life to take,
Mommy I just wanted it to be you and I,
not for me to die,
So I solidify your intentions
as I destroy your cervix like a T-Rex,
Wrap my umbilical cord around
the Doctor's trachea,
Eyes glazed over dark black

*like an evil doll's retina,
Covered in blood from the
extraction from your vagina,
Mommy you created me to destroy me
like a monster,
And toss me in a dumpster,
Hold still as I cauterize your eyes,
& demoralize you for all your lies,
As I lay to rest skin to skin as we both
die immortalized in deadly sin.*

Oct. 28th 2019

*Oct. 28th 2019
Excuse the sloppy penmanship Mom,
I can barely tell what planet that I'm on,
Twenty-two years since you've been gone,
Here I am still rambling on,
Too far gone since alcohol took my hand
a twenty-one, Chased my sorrows
in that bourbon, Withdrew into myself
and closed the curtains, My pity party had zero
invites to hide the hurting, I became someone I
didn't recognize a miserable person,
Scared me what I had become which made me
determined, To break the alcoholic cycle
before my eyes darken, I hope you're proud
because it was one of the hardest lessons*

that was worth learning. I love you Mom.

Inspire You

*I don't require the skill set
to be a qualifier,
I'm not the type of writer
that tries to inspire,
Waking up in a cold sweat,
lighten up a cigarette,
Drowned you out with a cassette,
songs all about regret,
Standing behind the television set
is a demon's silhouette,
Whiskey helps me forget,
a writer addicted to the alphabet,
Live-stream this shit on the internet,
me playing Russian roulette,
On your mark get set,
poetry has been my only outlet,
Before the dementia onset,
am I inspiring you yet?*

Immortal Love

*My skeletal frame remembers your name
Long after I'm buried away in my grave
And when the dust all settles down*

And the sunlight fades on autumn's ground
Till the leaves decay and blow to the wind
Till my grave stone breaks and new life begins
When my words survive the test of life's time
Until God decides Earth is to finally die
My love will live on forever for you
If life was too harsh and gently unfair
It was your love that made this journey clear
Opened my eyes to something brand new
Opened my heart to embrace you
Your beauty will always remain
In my mind till death retains
I'll love you way beyond forever and a day
And just a simple glance takes my breath away
So as we walk side by side till the end
Our love will live on
and be whispered in the wind.

Should Be Famous

Hello I'm brainless,
There's no reason I should be famous,
Since mental illness isn't contagious,
My parents are blameless,
Drugs made their lives fucking painless,
Yet I'm the ignoramus.

Streaming

I'd like to take a hiatus from streaming,
My creativity seems to be depleting,
Take a year off of Instagram & Facebook,
& bury my face in a good book,
Cancel Netflix, Hulu, Disney+ & Vudu,
Drift through novels and stories I didn't get to.

Thought Otherwise

What a conundrum,
a scoundrel locked the fair maiden
away in a dungeon,
A pungent smell of booze reeked off
the man named Hughes,
The fair maiden made a breakthrough,
Secretly the scoundrel was the Father
she never knew,
Locked in restrains of his oblivious sins,
The maiden freed herself
with a heirloom hair pin,
Adamantly she sought out his allusive love,
"Father why do you hate me so,
why was I disposed of"
Until the horrific tragedy of her early demise,
That fateful day opened up his eyes,
He finally kissed his Daughter

and tried to emphasize,
"Daughter I love you"
unfortunately she and Death thought otherwise.

Mom's Pregnancy

At age 13 found out
about my Mom's pregnancy,
Hit me emotionally thought she
was replacing me,
She proceeded to move away
with her new family,
2 hours away without me
because my Dad had custody,
Poor wittle me grow up
you don't need your Mommy,
You're turning 14 finally friends
and a girlfriend so whoopee,
Then disaster struck me
like a nightmare ensnared me,
Mom had died permanently leaving me,
I'm 37 and I still dream about
how she abandoned me,
No closure just regret and uncertainly.

Bully Immunity

It's not currently PC but back in the 90's,

As a kid I wish I could've executed
my bullies on their knees,
Smile as I give the trigger a squeeze,
And leave their brains splattered
like some zombies,
But in 2019 society gives immunity
to these bullies,
Blame it on a learning deficiency
or dysfunctional families,
And ignore the torment
that fucking happened to me.

North Face

"That guy looks weird,
look at his homeless man beard,
If he jumped off the train platform
people would've cheered,
The world would be better off if he disappeared."

"You pretentious North Face® bitches
sipping your Starbucks,
Your husbands probably face down
in his secretary's muff,
Your meager existence delegates
that I give zero fucks."

Cupcakes

There's a plethora of heartbreak,
Tales of heartache, Jesus for fuck's sake,
I've got a bellyache; I ate too many cupcakes.

Silhouettes of the Forgotten

A desert of silhouettes of forgotten friends
Rising up from the smoke into the light
My once inner circle of unmasked characters
My perception of our past travels haunts me
I feel the absence of your lights in my life
Abandoned by choices I've made selfishly
Ignorant to the cries of joy and sadness
Our harmony burnt away to mere ashes
My purpose leading to rivalry and spite
Managing time and again with duct tape repairs
I acknowledge this conclusion of friendships
Beginning and ending in life's sparse moments
My last attempt to heal these old wounds
And repair those damages left in my path
The old film strip plays on in silence
While the picture frames just dissolve away

Someday

Someday I'll be dead, Oh,

I'll be gone from this world,
Just a gravesite,
With no significant mark on this world.

Halloween Night

The projection screen shows a grieving teen,
Attending his Mother's wake on Halloween.

Keep My Composure

I've been isolating myself
long before Covid-19,
A suicidal teen looking
at a blank computer screen,
I was 16,
had my heart ripped out by the Prom Queen,
Her AOL screen-name: "It's over.
Full disclosure,
I'm cheating on you."
Writing back trying to keep my composure,
Fuck you Bitch I wouldn't
"check you out" if I was your fucking Grocer,
I'll pop up in your nightmares
like a homicidal gopher,
I'd approach her,
call her a fucking Katie Holmes poseur,
Trust me you don't want this kind of exposure,

*I'm the kind of crazy Britney Spears
couldn't get over.*

Amniotic Sac

*Busting out of an amniotic sac,
Doctor's trying to force me back,
"The World Fucking Hates You",
Well I'm alright with that.*

Family Normalcy

*Finding it hard just to concentrate,
I still reside in a broken home
I can't vacate,
You can't relate since
your parent's marriage was so great,
They'd never separate since
they loved their little ingrate,
But drugs obliviate family
normalcy and incinerate,
Those comfy cozy warm feelings that
happiness use to create.*

Pushing Keys

*FUCKIN' nobody pushes more KEYS than me,
I'm Keyboard fiend addicted to obscene Poetry,*

Impulse control disorder,
making my SHIT List shorter,
Alphabetically find your name,
apply "Fuck You" it's all the same,
As I'm spewing chunks on stage,
a thespian trying to act my age.

No Fly List

Fuck, I've got the Coronavirus
from Miley Cyrus,
Looking like Death just like Osiris,
Even got me on that No Fly List.

Disorderly Teen

Isolated worse than when I was 13,
A fucking Pandemic they call it COVID-19,
Crawling the fucking walls
like I was a disorderly teen,
In quarantine sealed up
like a pristine copy of Amazing Fantasy #15,
Music to Be Murdered By
seems to be my only vaccine,
Surviving on junk food
you'd find in a vending machine.

Cobwebs and Dust

Trudging through the past,
our memories are permanently stashed,
In the attic covered in cobwebs,
dust and whatever we had last,
Whether it was love, heartache,
lies or betrayals, it all smashed,
Boxed up little disclaimer fragile
waiting someday to be trashed.

Mandolorian

According to this accordion,
I'm time skipping in my DeLorean,
Almost 40 and wannabe a good Dad
like the Mandolorian.

Experiment with Cocaine

To eradicate this pain,
should I experiment with Cocaine,
Codeine, will it constrain the demons enchained,
In my brain, should I abstain from this profane
language I use to explain,
Sever my jugular vein,
leaving a bloodstain to get
your attention again.

Cuentos De La Familia

My cousin fell for this chick
He felt euphoria when she held him close
His Heroine that eased the childhood abuse away
Injecting him with a spellbinding love
That he'd overdose on; Ms. Heroin

My Mama was suggestive to booze
Pouring Carlo Rossi into a Big Gulp cup
Slurring speech face down on the kitchen table
Curled up on the rug for the duration
For the rest of my weekend visitation

Bunghole

"We gather here to mourn the passing of…"
Pop out my casket like "Fucking Hello",
Did you miss me, I'm an Asshole,
Fuckin' Lexapro had total control,
You're about to feel the wrath
of my almighty bunghole.

Quarantine

"In the midst of this Quarantine,
where the fucks Captain Planet
and those stupid teens?",

Relax, don't panic, pop a handful of Xanax,
he's over there in the hammock,
Drinking a Margarita Pomegranate being served by that Green Deal fanatic,
"Is that AOC going down on him like the Titanic?",
Avert your eyes; it's a bit anticlimactic,
For her draining the Planet,
She uses Tide PODS® to cleanse her palate.

Nitrous Oxide

Every time those thoughts of suicide,
Creep in I inhale this Nitrous oxide,
Deep inside 'til those thought subside.

COVID-19

Instead of spreading COVID-19,
we're spreading L.O.V.E.,
As the World's isolating itself in quarantine,
We can still connect via tech like LiveJournal,
Whether it's Tiger King,
Animal Crossing, Zoom or Doom Eternal,
You might be Home Alone
but let's celebrate today,
Throwing a righteous House Party
just like Kid and Play,
Even if it's hard to stay in

with this absolutely perfect weather.
If we Stay Home, Stay Safe
we'll get through this together.

World's Greatest Dad

My parents liked to gobble up drugs,
Wake up on rugs;
give your heart strings a tug,
Put some codeine in a
"World's Greatest Dad" mug.

My Sensei

What's my pen say,
dispatch you like my sensei,
A bad effing hombre
spilling your effing latte,
Amscray, I'm Lit AF,
you're just a butt in an ashtray.

Augmenting History

Hooked up to an intravenous drip
with phencyclidine,
Hallucinating a horrific scene,
an adamant teen in a time machine,
Rebuking Death by putting his skull head

under a guillotine,
Four days late on Halloween,
Augmenting history in my explicit memory,
Mom's still dead from Heart Failure;
I've failed to save her,
I'll recalculate tomorrow and relentlessly
try to be her savior.

The Mirror Monster

Does the liquor conjure up the specter of her?
Say her name 3x's in the mirror
to reveal a Monster,
Your sister you hated,
spread lies and conjecture,
I picture you're ashamed
and don't want any exposure,
But consider I'm bitter 'cause she's my Mother,
So I'm the inner voice whispering
"Aren't you the real Monster?"

Bleaker

In Fall of '00 my life was much bleaker
blasting heavy metal music from a speaker,
Punk rocker t-shirt with black Converse sneakers,
Cocky demeanor, in my heart a believer,
Always labeled an underachiever,

although I passed on the reefer,
Fuck my Poetry Teacher creeping around
just like a creature,
"You're not using the proper procedure;
your poetry's too dark",
But I can go deeper, into childhood traumas
Lifetime wouldn't feature,
Death of my Mother, the alcohol,
drugs and childhood I could never recover,
Divorce and fits of rage
as my Mother's boyfriend would shove her,
"Can you write happiness?"
Did I just fucking st-st-stutter?
This mother fucker abused my Mother and you want
happy Poetry let me slip on this rubber,
'Cause I'm about to fuck up this poem
'cause I'm Getting Too Old For This Shit
like Danny Glover.

Happy and Content

I reside in your heart, happy and content,
Singing aloud about the day that we met,
Your eyes caused my itty bitty heart to augment,
I was yours from the start with no argument,

'Till you closed off the valves causing disorient,
Flooding the heart chamber with torment,

Noxious gas occupying my lungs so maleficent,
Our love became fatal was that your intent?

Liquid Cyanide

By the by;
have you tried this liquid Cyanide,
Give it a try;
leave viewers horrified by your suicide.

Fidget Spinners

I'll solicit a ticket,
a snippet of wicked,
Hold on to your spinner
incase if you fidget,
Granny's homemade chicken and biscuits,
And a couple of misfits,
little delinquents,
Bullying my mom constantly
little half wits,
'Til her mom confronted
these little cunt shits,
Challenged them to fight my mom
one on one just fists,
My mom smashed these little bitches
like Halloween pumpkins,
Story told round the world

like a fucking Yo-Yo by Duncan®.

Oregon Trail

"Do you have butterflies in your stomach?"

No, it's more like a hive of bees
inside an autumn tree dropping leaves,
Or breaking out in hives
from insecticides
leaving me half paralyzed,
Or dying from pneumonia
playing Oregon Trail on a PC in Oklahoma.
Tombstone read dunce without a diploma.

Free Spirit

she's a free spirit
that dances in the rain.

she's comfortable
in being spontaneous.

fuck that shit,
i'm not a sell out.

Mermaid Lagoon

*Underneath a starry sky,
on the shore of a mermaid lagoon,
We consummate our love,
underneath a bright crescent moon.*

R.I.P Chester

*I had a heavy pain deep inside my soul,
Depression unfortunately had taken hold,
And a frequently listened to this CD,
Linkin Park's Hybrid Theory,
So thank you Chester Bennington,
For your music helped heal a bit of me.*

Warmth of the Sun

*The warmth of the sun
would fill this room so long ago
with laughter and life so long ago.
So many smiling faces as
you were embraced by loved ones
as you entered so long ago.
But the light doesn't filter
through any longer, this room is empty now,
and there isn't anything but
memories that linger. All the parties,*

*all the talks, all the childhood
memories are just echoes
that reverberates inside of my mind.
And I may be the last one here,
holding back tears; I miss them all
and it'll never feel the same.*

Bartender's Request

*she drowned her regret in a
martini glass until the
bartender said, "get the fuck out".*

Been Suicidal

I've been suicidal since I reversed the vinyl.

Spelling Tests

*I must confess, I didn't possess
the finesse from transferring from CPS,
I became friendless and you can bear witness
at every recess, My dialect and dress,
the Suburban kids considered a mess,
Nevertheless, being bullied became
routine more or less, And all that hatred
they spewed I couldn't digest, So I
allowed my inner demons to manifest,*

*Fuck my teachers and the fucking
spelling tests, My classmates can finally
witness a Catholic schoolboy possessed.*

Go to Work

*Mom had to go to work,
And family wouldn't watch me,
Mom had to go to work,
So off to a drug addict's house,
Mom had to go to work,
Hated every fucking minute,
Mom had to go to work,
Till this day I'll never forget it.*

Burning Wildly

*Tell me you're so proud of me,
As gasoline is doused on me,
Strike a match and set fire to me,
Burning wildly are you watching me,
Raising flames say your goodbyes to me.*

Little Sour Tart

*In Art, I'd doodle "I Love You"
on construction paper hearts,
You'd crumple them up or rip them apart,*

I wish you were sweeter my little sour tart,
Cause when we're older
you might regret you broke my heart.

TMZ

TMZ commandeered my sex tape
with Britney Spears,
Back before her fucking career disappeared,
…Baby One More Time
took me a few souvenirs,
Her Crossroads panties and her
Mouseketeer Mouse Ears.

Poltergeist

"Let's check your mental health."

Doc, I fucking hate myself,
Even helped the poltergeist
knock shit off my shelf.

Foghorn Leghorn

Psychologist: Please,
start from the beginning.

Me: It's frighten but let's dive in,

I was the 1st born riding a one horned unicorn,
Airborne until I was grounded for watching porn,
Pop the popcorn; I'm loud mouth'd
like Foghorn Leghorn.

Poison Ivy

Promise me you'll always love me,
She said as she fucking killed me,
Burying me where nobody
would ever find me,
In a shallow grave
covered by poison ivy.

Spread Lies

A few years after my Momma died,
Her boyfriend spread lies
like it was a homicide,
Which coincide with him
attempting to kidnap my half-brother
before he was identified,
School went on lockdown
as the authorities were notified,
I could breathe a sigh his plot
was foiled before he could retry,
So in my kindest words, "Fuck that guy!"

Unshaven

I'm an unshaven Caucasian
suffering from sleep deprivation,
Off medication misbehaving like
my mind's a safe haven for Satan.

Threw Us Together

Thought we'd all be
"Best Friends Forever",
However…
it became quite the endeavor,
Life threw us all together,
And for whatever reasons life
became so much better,
I remember you all felt
like family members,
And I never expected it to become
us parting ways forever.

Marker

You Xed out your Ex & called them a
Mother Fucker,
Yet that X on your Ex is erasable
Not Marker.

Troll Me

*She said "I was her one & only",
But then she dethroned me,
Had her friends troll me & Rick Roll me,
Ate sweets & I became a Roly-Poly,
Singing "Ravioli ravioli,
give me the formu-oli".*

Invisible Cloak

*It would've been so dope
to have an invisible cloak,
I'd a been super stoked to avoid the bully's
unprovoked insulting joke,
Shove an artichoke down his fucking throat,
have him croak.*

Connoisseur

*I'm pretty sure if I won the lotto
I wouldn't become a connoisseur,
I'd probably detour
and pour a pile of manure
at your domicile because I'm that immature,
post a sign saying
"Don't say I never gave you shit",
with a cape so you can be Super Mad*

while throwing a fit.

Final Poem

*An exhausting yawn,
on a bright green lawn,
Illuminated by moonlight
hours before dawn,
The magnificent moon
encompasses the night sky,
Comfort in that sometime soon,
I'll reunite with you,
Goody-bye.*